THE
TRUMP
PROPHECIES

UPDATED AND EXPANDED

THE
TRUMP
PROPHECIES

THE ASTONISHING TRUE STORY OF THE MAN WHO
SAW TOMORROW...AND WHAT HE SAYS IS

COMING NEXT

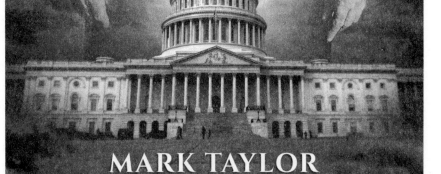

MARK TAYLOR

Defender

Crane, MO

The Trump Prophecies: The Astonishing True Story of the Man Who Saw Tomorrow...and What He Says Is Coming Next: UPDATED AND EXPANDED

Defender
Crane, MO 65633
©2019 by Mark Taylor
All rights reserved. Published 2019.
Printed in the United States of America.

ISBN: 978-1-9480142-1-2
A CIP catalog record of this book is available from the Library of Congress.

Cover illustration and design by Jeffrey Mardis.

STOP!

Before you proceed in this book, please note that this is the updated and revised edition of *The Trump Prophecies*, which was initially published in 2017. The original release covered the story of how firefighter Mark Taylor's extraordinary "Commander-In-Chief Prophecy" rightly predicted Donald Trump's against-all-odds presidential victory in 2016, as well as the additional prophecies Mark wrote regarding what would take place in the United States following Trump's astounding win.

Since the first edition hit the shelves, the number of accurately forecast post-election developments Mark formerly revealed have stacked, requiring a modified release that revisits these events.

If read from beginning to end—without an understanding of this revision's layout—this book holds the potential of confusing the reader since the author's voice switches from Mark Taylor to the publisher's additions. As you read on, you will notice text set apart with lines above and below and a different font. This stylistic change represents the updated sections, provided to you by Defender Publishing.

Contents

Foreword

———

Today is February 4, 2019. I—Donna Howell, managing editor here at Defender Publishing—am still good friends with Mark Taylor, and I keep up with him fairly frequently. I know him better now than when I wrote the foreword to the first edition of his book several years ago, and I can tell you that my glowing first impression of Mark was dead-on accurate.

I have a few words to say since getting to know Mark better, but rather than to strike my initial impression (captured here in this original foreword) I will preserve it here, so readers can be reminded of what my earliest thoughts were about the man who wrote the "Commander-in-Chief Prophecy." That makes my current understanding of Mark Taylor, the man—as opposed to Mark Taylor, the prophet—all the more powerful. I will catch up with you readers for a brief, personal update at the end of the foreword. First, however, here is the piece I wrote for the front of *The Trump Prophecies* in July of 2017:

———

My name is Donna Howell. I was hired alongside Allie Anderson to help piece together the research and outline plan for this book.

I remember the day I was told I'd be flying to Florida to interview Mark Taylor—the man who played such an active role in the incredible election of 2016. I try never to allow myself to develop preconceived ideas about people, but I had heard of this prophecy writer, and despite myself, I had an idea about who I was going to meet. I imagined a vociferous and booming man in a suit with a hundred apocalyptic verses from Revelation just waiting to fall out of his mouth after a hearty—but serious—handshake.

When Allie and I settled into our hotel, we met at the diner downstairs to gather our thoughts. We walked past the reserved SkyWatch TV conference room and took a selfie for kicks, having absolutely no idea what the conversation in those walls would reveal less than twenty-four hours later. Armed with a good night's sleep and a fully charged laptop battery, Allie and I were just pulling our chairs up to the table in the conference room when we saw a shadow fall upon the door.

"Looks like I'm in the right place," the man said.

Allie stood and held her hand out to greet him. "Mark Taylor?" she asked.

"That's me," Mark said with a smile. His unassuming and relaxed posture, coupled with the casual khaki pants and blue polo shirt, immediately let us know that he was as personable and unpretentious as they come.

Needless to say, meeting Mark in person made the suit-man with the loud voice and forceful persona concepts fly out the window of my mind. I leaned over the table and shook Mark's hand, introduced myself, and then returned to my chair. I poured us all a glass of ice water as I listened to Mark describing his drive over. His southern accent and calm demeanor offered an easy segue way into his life story—which was followed by his message to the Church and the citizens of our country.

…Wow.

In our line of work, Allie and I have heard a lot of doom-and-gloom messages of terror. We've learned over the course of time to take it all with a grain of salt and keep plodding on, believing that God is ultimately in control. But Mark's aim for sharing what the Lord has given him to say doesn't resemble anything I've ever seen or heard. I didn't want to derail his momentum with an occasionally disruptive "Amen!" so I just kept quiet and calm and took lots of careful notes. Inside, however, I was buzzing with excitement, and, based on the expression Allie had on her face for most of the meeting (as well as her own comments later that evening), she felt the same.

It was so refreshing to see a man as humble and sincere as Mark Taylor approach the will and spoken words of God with such zeal, but what really hit Allie and I both was the *positivity* of what he had to say. It's not about blood moons or the Illuminati or the end of the world. It's about revival amidst the remnant in the Church and a Great Awakening for the lost all over the globe!

I am grateful that Tom Horn asked Mark to share his thoughts with this country through this book, and I truly believe its readers will be inspired and revitalized toward a united Kingdom goal as a result.

————

In the time that I've been honored to call Mark Taylor a friend, I have observed him shrinking as far away from the limelight as possible, never wanting attention or glory. He maintains integrity under unimaginable pressures, and despite opposition, he humbly plods ahead, determined to remain willing (like the prophets of old) to be obedient to the Lord in carrying His warnings to His people. The tenacity that Mark has harnessed while walking such an uncomfortable path has been an inspiration to everyone here at Defender Publishing and SkyWatch Television, and I don't think it's a stretch to say that Mark Taylor is a kind of hero to us all.

Although I'm not always shocked when someone proves over time that their sincerity and reliability is just what they represented it to be in the beginning, the same cannot be said of my expectations regarding a prophet's words or ideas. With my personal exposure to countless false prophets throughout my life, I have grown to anticipate failed predictions. I'm generally only surprised when a prophet's words turn out to be true, and even then I can usually chalk it up to coincidence when the prophecy was generic enough to be interpreted a number of different ways.

Mark, however, has been a complete anomaly to us all. He doesn't give vague predictions that "could mean a number of different things depending on the reader." Much to the contrary, when he writes down a word from the Lord, Mark lists very specific events that will transpire, how and when they will occur, and what people will be involved. Such precision can't be faked, and basic knowledge of mathematics proves this isn't luck or coincidence. We here at Defender Publishing have watched, amazed, as global episodes have played out just as Prophet Mark Taylor have said they would—

...Over and over and over again.

In the words of SkyWatch TV and Defender Publishing's CEO, Tom Horn, "Mark Taylor is, so far, batting a thousand!"

It simply didn't seem logical that we wouldn't revise *The Trump Prophecies* for our readers to shed light on what has happened since the beginning of this astounding journey. Therefore, without further ado, Defender Publishing presents to you: *The Trump Prophecies: The Astonishing True Story of the Man Who Saw Tomorrow...and What He Says Is Coming Next: UPDATED AND EXPANDED.*

———

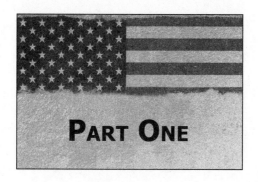

PART ONE

The Man

The Voice

It was Thursday, April, 28. The year was 2011. The clock attested that it was well past dinner.

I was sitting in my living room absent-mindedly flipping through the channels on my television. I had little care for the images and sounds that were flooding out of that fifty-inch, flat-screen entertainment box and into my consciousness as my body was slowly becoming one with the fluff of my recliner. My brain was now an impenetrable wall over which very little incoming information could overcome as my body was deteriorating and my mind was its most recent victim. Reflections and feelings within me had turned into an unrecognizable pool of negative jelly over the last several years—all cognitive capabilities gradually succumbing to the power of demoralizing depression. I was no longer able, as I once was, to "look on the bright side" or see the positive aspects of life since the sickness had gripped me. Everywhere I looked, all was lost, and the only lifesaver floating on my waters anymore was the promise I had from the Lord that I was loved and that He was in control.

For as long as I live, I will never forget the torment of those miserable years. I was fading into a shell of a person, existing as a useless puddle of nausea and dizziness, while most days I lacked even the strength to rise from my bed or even read. My stomach was wrecked, my muscles were atrophied, and my thoughts were a confusing paradox of roadblocks that clouded all normalcy. The world around me was spinning away. My grasp on reality was blurring into a canvas of dark colors that bled into unconstructive patterns of weary desperation that left my spirit staggering and lost in my own brand of wilderness.

I was sick.

I was deflated.

I was *dying*...

And Fox News was merely the ambient imagery that gave me something to stare at while I wasted away.

Well beyond me at that point was the concept that I would be of use in the Kingdom of God in my current state. That God could use an uneducated sick man at death's door to accomplish anything would be a feat larger than that which I could wrap my mind around as I stood at the threshold of giving up all hope entirely. The vision I had of me writing on my bedroom floor remained largely unlocked by this time, so any concepts of my communing with the Holy Spirit as a messenger of the Lord's for the nation was obsolete.

But then it happened. The moment that altered the course of my life. That moment—in 2011, sitting in front of my television in my cream-colored living room—that everything changed...

In the unlikeliest of ways and from the unlikeliest angle.

I saw Donald Trump's face come on the air, and although I had seen him in the media hundreds of times prior and never thought a thing about it, something deep within my spirit immediately snapped to awareness...like an invisible sergeant within the Army of the Lord calling me to attention. A signal had finally penetrated the static interference that my spiritual radars had become. The fog lifted. My perception became alert and ready to receive. My discernment soared off the charts!

Though my life in those days were frequently haunted by my physical inability to even rise from my bed, I now understand why the Lord allowed me the extra energy to plant my feet on that tan-carpeted floor and stand to hear the voice behind the microphone. It wasn't what Trump was saying in his address about international currencies, it was the frequency that he was emulating that harmonized with a Holy Spirit-led call for me, Mark Taylor, to respond. For a brief few seconds, I allowed the Spirit to weave together the connecting threads between the man on the screen and the enigmatic message blaring within me like a siren louder than any I'd known in my career as a fireman. An epiphany of truth with the most evident clarity rooted me to the floor as I heard the Lord speak…

You are hearing the voice of a president.

With newfound determination, I made my way to my office and sat down at my desk. I listened as the Spirit gave me the words to write, never once comprehending the impact it would have on the globe in the short years that followed.

I am Mark Taylor, author of the "Commander-in-Chief Prophecy," and this is my story and message to the Church.

chapter one

Firefighting

Ialways wanted to be a fireman. The dream was not one born out of whims of fancy, but of watching the deeds of the fireman who had gone before me in my family line. My grandfather, "Pops" as we called him, had been a firefighter, as had been my immediate father. The work of a fireman is hard and demanding on both body and mind, and requires only the utmost diligence to continue with success as we continuously report to work for those stressful and lengthy twenty-four-hour shifts.

From my earliest days, I knew that being in this field wasn't anything like the romanticized image the books and movies painted it to be: four men in red rubber suits and helmets drinking coffee, playing poker, and smoking cigars while waiting for a bell to ring; enjoying the fun swirly-ride down the steel pole between the upper and lower floors when called to action; and then wandering into burning buildings for five minutes with a hose and emerging as heroes holding grateful, weeping damsels in ash-stained dresses. No. I knew what the fire stations and staff *really* looked like: weary bodies on uncomfortable cots hoping to catch a few minutes of sleep before the bell yanks them from their slumber so they can report for duty at scenes of tragic injury, knife wounds, car accidents, pools of blood, people trapped in flaming buildings, physical altercations…and frequently, death, when even the most efficient rescue attempts don't make it in time.

Nevertheless, I knew if Dad could do it, and if Pops could do it, I could do my part in preserving lives as well, and I was determined to. Besides, it wasn't only my close proximity to tragedy through their line of work that had taught me about the fragility of life. From my very birth, there were other serious complications.

I was born in 1966, during the days of "twilight sleep" child-birthing methods wherein the laboring birth mother was tied to the bed with lamb's wool straps and constantly drugged. Women back then would go into the hospital in labor and be administered a combination of morphine and scopolamine, which was believed at the time to bring the mother into a sleep state during which her body would continue to contract and cooperate with the birthing experience, but supposedly her mind would be at peace in the drug-induced "happy place," or so it was advertised. Many women came out of the hospitals in those days not remembering a thing—they would simply recall going in pregnant, and come out the next day with a baby.

Would that my mother had only been one of those women who fell into the happy state of twilight sleep and emerged the next day with a baby! But that wasn't the case for her.

I am not certain of the medicines administered to Mom at the time of my birth, my mother still remembers a very nasty nurse forcing drugs down her throat and into her nasal passages to the point that it gagged her, and she was unable to defend herself, as she was bound to the birthing bed. I was in the birth canal for *three days* while this went on, and it felt like an eternity to her. Studies have since shown that the combination of certain drugs and a prolonged delay in the narrow birth canal (especially when the baby is repeatedly cut off from either oxygen or a steady flow of amniotic fluids, her water having broken three days prior) can cause all kinds of birth defects, including mental disabilities. By the grace of God, and that alone, I somehow managed to be one of the lucky ones to escape unscathed. When my birth finally heralded an end to Mom's torture, the trauma of it all resulted in an enormous and painful tear down her leg.

Though I would not assume that every distressful birthing scenario automatically means the enemy is attempting to keep someone from being born or causing them to be born with defects, I definitely believe in my case that Satan never wanted me to see the world.

I had terrible nightmares as a child. Following my own "crib death" (now known as "Sudden Infant Death Syndrome") at around seven weeks old—the day I was inexplicably revived when my panicked father grabbed me—I lived in fear of sleep through most of my earliest years. My nightmares were so ghoulish and petrifying that seeking reassurance from my mother became a part of my nightly routine.

"Mommy, am I gonna have a bad dream?"

"No, sweetie. You are *not* going to have a bad dream."

It was an exchange that absolutely had to happen before I would surrender to the temptation of sleep that tugged at my eyelids each night. But although my mother's words comforted me past the initial concern, there were, unfortunately, many manifested nightmares that took hold of my imagination before the sun would rise. Little did I know at the time, dreams, both good and bad, would remain an important part of my life.

When I wasn't suffering from the frequent high fevers I had so often when I was little, lethargically watching episodes of my favorite television show *Emergency*, I would play "fire engines" with the neighbor boy. My house was located in a subdivision of Orlando, Florida, around apartments and commercial buildings, but the area was open and had long stretches of grassy yards. I had a Tonka firetruck with an extension ladder, and my friend had one that would connect to a garden hose. Between the two of us, we spent oh-so-many hours putting on our "fireman suits" (standard outdoor coats) and "responding" to all the emergencies we could dream up, hosing down all the "burning buildings" (bushes, weeds, mailboxes) of the backyard. I was largely the one with real-world intel, so I played a big role in determining the outcomes of our games.

Eventually, the area where we lived developed into somewhat of a ghetto. Crime mounted, and we faced several home robberies, so we moved to Orlando's east side. It was there that I entered junior high, but when my mind was not required to focus on schooling, I was either dreaming of fire stations or spending time with my Pops.

Most of my childhood, Pops was my father figure. My Dad was an incredible provider who always took his jobs seriously, working two or three at a time, but he was so tremendously stressed from the demands of his work (demands that I now understand quite personally) that he could be hard to get along with at times, and he was rarely home. My sister Ashley and I, as well as my mother, knew Dad loved us a great deal, but because of his absence and recurrent mood swings, Ashley and I considered Pops a father figure. (Note that this is no longer the case. After facing my own years as a fireman, the relationship between Dad and me has been restored, and any relational bumps from those earlier years have been dealt with and left in the past.)

Pops would come and pick me up quite often—usually every Saturday—and we would drive around, go to his house to work on various projects, and hang around in his RV, where he would tell me stories of his days as a firefighter in London, England, during the World War II era. Sometimes he would take me camping in the woods, and those are memories I deeply cherish. I could talk to that man about anything, and he always seemed to have just the right advice. No juvenile phase of mine intimidated him from being the sound counselor I needed. But more than just being the quintessential wisdom-giver, Pops was a friend. His smile and laughter had a way of stomping down my adolescent anxieties and helped pull me out of any funk, and I valued his company more than anyone my own age. On any given day, I preferred watching him work with his hands and listening to the events of his life to seeing other junior-highers act hip and get into trouble. As a preacher, he proved knowledgeable about the Word of God as well, and stood as a godly example for me when moral conundrums posed difficult decisions.

Pops' father was also a preacher who helped plant a few churches in the Orlando area and evangelized in the mountains of North Carolina and Tennessee, spreading the Gospel by foot. (It skipped a generation with my Dad, who never became a minister, but I have since had dreams confirming that the mantle Pops held has come to me in my prophetic ministry.) So Pops' stories reflected a life not wasted, and there was something about his living testimony that drew me in and made me resolved not to waste mine.

I wish I could have had him around for another thirty years, as I was about to enter a challenging era, but sadly it was not to be.

In my final year attending high school in East Orlando, just two weeks before graduation, I began night school at the Fire Academy, enrolled in a sixteen-week program. At about week fourteen, I decided to take a break from preparing for all my upcoming final exams by assisting Pops in another of our projects. We worked to remove the seats from Dad's new bass fishing boat and carried each of them to my car to have them reupholstered. It was August, and the weather was blistering, especially in the open sun near the barn where we were laboring away. When the final seat had been hauled to my car, I got in to drive the seats to the upholstery place and started a short conversation with Pops out the window.

Suddenly, he leaned over and grabbed the car for support. I knew immediately that something was wrong. My Fire Academy training was racing through my head as I assessed the situation and attempted to take control.

"What's wrong, Pops?" I said, getting out of the car and running to his side.

"I don't feel good."

"Well, you probably got too hot. Come back to the barn and cool off a bit."

Initially Pops listened to my advice, but the moment I had him sitting on a bench in the shade, he insisted I take him to his truck. Looking back, considering how well he recognized the symptoms of death through his experience in WWII, I think he knew what was about to happen, and he wanted to avoid it happening in front of me or Ashley, who was just inside the house. I imagine his plan was to drive to the hospital alone, so as not to worry the rest of us, and if he found himself unable to continue the drive, at least he could pull over and fall into rest without allowing us to see him suffer.

"Pops," I argued, "just try to cool off a little bit. Just sit there and be still for a minute and cool off. Okay? Please, Pops, just rest a minute."

But my plea was no longer effective.

"Mark, take me to my truck. I want to go to my truck."

Reluctantly, I agreed to help him get to his vehicle…and I would come to regret that decision for a great number of years.

Just as I hoisted him to stand, he collapsed unconscious in my arms. Instantly, I lowered him to the ground and began CPR. Mom saw this from the house and came running out to the barn in a panic. I yelled for her to get a rescue truck on the way, and within minutes she had made the call and returned to assist me. I gave compressions while my mother gave mouth-to-mouth. When we saw the EMS down the road, we ran out to flag them down and then continued CPR on Pops until the crew was ready to move in and take over. I prayed fervently as I watched them load my father figure into that truck and made my way to the hospital behind them.

Of all the moments in my life when my training and preparation did not result in a saved life, this was the most heartbreaking for me. Nana, Pops' wife, came to me when we had received the news that he was gone. She cried as she thanked me for trying to save him, but it didn't change the fact that I would have to live knowing I had been unsuccessful.

Pops' death had an enormous impact on my sister, Ashley, and me. Life took a turn in one day. Ashley was fifteen years old when she watched my mom and me desperately performing CPR to save him, and much anxiety and depression was the result of such a traumatic experience. From that moment to this day, my sister has relied on me to help fill the void left by Pops' passing. There have been days in Ashley's life when she felt so alone that I dropped everything I was doing to be with her and see her through the challenges she faced. Her testimony is her own, so I will let her be the one to share it, but needless to say, Pops' death was an intense and drastic event that led to much mourning and grief. I wish he could have seen some of the things I've done with my life here on earth, and there have been many instances I wished he had been around to provide what was always the wisest of counsel.

Oh, the camping trips we could have had just after the Lord gave me my first prophetic charge…

Nevertheless, Pops is now walking pain-free on the streets of gold with Jesus, so I am thankful I have a reunion to look forward to someday.

After graduating from the Fire Academy in 1986, I was hired on at the Orlando Fire Department, and my first shift was Christmas Day. I served at the busiest stations downtown for about eight months until I requested a transfer to Station Two (in the ghettos), where my help was needed the most. The biggest engine company in the city was Engine 2, the one I was assigned to. That station received twelve thousand calls per year. I knew before I transferred that it would be a tough place, but it was essential that the high-crime areas had devoted responders, and I knew Pops would be proud of me if he could see how seriously I was taking my position. My expectations of chaos were met—and exceeded—with more stabbings, cuttings, shootings, cardiac arrests, traffic accidents, and fires than I could count. You name it, we ran it, and for many calls there was a verbal or physical confrontation that we fireman were pulled into when we arrived on the scene. The station was in a frenzy twenty-four hours per day, seven days a week, for all the years I worked there. An eight-foot chain-link fence with barbed wire circling the top kept the property looking like a prison, and any time the crew was away on a call (which was pretty much always), the station was on lockdown. However, there was always "that one fireman" last out of the building who would forget to lock the door, and we would arrive back to find the homeless sleeping in our cots and using our toothbrushes (among a few other unpleasant occurrences).

Any time multiple calls rang in to report the same fire from different angles, we knew it was more than a couple of teenagers roasting hot dogs over a barbecue grill. Multiple calls meant that a legitimate fire was in progress and lives were potentially in danger. One of these instances involved reports of a little boy trapped in a house. From six blocks away as we loaded into the truck, I could see the smoke billowing up into the sky, and although I had received "someone's trapped in a building" calls before that had turned out to be false alarms, something in my gut told me that this time it was legitimate. As quickly as we were moving as professional and expedient responders, it still felt as if we couldn't get there fast enough, and I was concerned.

Engine 2 was the first to arrive, and everyone on my truck immediately took to their positions as the fire blew out into the street. My engine's job was to hold the fire back and fight it down as much as possible until the truck company keyed in to perform a search for anyone still inside. I masked up, grabbed a one-and-three-quarter-inch hose, and ran to the back. People were screaming all around me, confirming that the child was still inside awaiting rescue. From the water's contact, black smoke hurled outward toward me. So much blackness surrounded me that I couldn't even see the fire. I could hear it crackling all around me, but all I could see was endless smoke. I had no choice but to press on, so even without visibility I just pushed my way in and through, spraying everywhere until I hit a window. I vented the hose for a split second near the glass to catch a quick glimpse of where I was at in the house (a technique that fireman are trained to use in instances of low visibility), and then continued toward the front door.

The truck was issuing its loud water-pumping hum as usual, boards were falling all around me, fire was popping from every direction, glass was shattering, firemen were yelling various communications through their masks, air horns and sirens were blaring from the incoming units, my hose was blasting its noisy spray—all the standard noises on the ground that I was accustomed to hearing—and I could still hear the mother of the boy screaming from outside.

As soon as the fire was out at the front, I vented the hose at the window for visibility again and turned for the remaining rooms as the other arriving responders began kicking through the glass and breaking their way into the house to search the burned zones.

That's when we finally found the child, on his knees in the bedroom of a burned zone. He had died perched at the window awaiting help. I will not describe what I saw when I looked at him, as it is a deeply disturbing and haunting image, but it was immediately clear that the little boy had been gone for a while.

It was the kind of thing we saw often in my line of work, and death was all around me constantly. Tragedy, trauma, injury, violence, and death. Around the clock. Every shift.

I actually counted once—six cuttings, two shootings, and at least two stabbings—all in one work day. On another occasion, we received sixteen emergency calls by three o'clock in the afternoon, five more by 9:30 p.m., and another eight by one o'clock in the morning, adding up to a total of twenty-nine emergency responses on a single shift. And, of course, there was frequently aggression from the victims against us as well, whether in the midst of a vicious riot or upon pulling a substance-abuser from a fire. Many times, the victims had no idea of what was happening around them, because they were so intoxicated or high on dope that they would have sat right there in the flames or the violence until their life was ended—and all they saw when I was wrapping my arms around them and removing them from danger was another antagonist who needed to be fought or verbally assaulted.

In the early 1990s, I decided to become a fire engineer (the driver of the firetruck), so I took the exam and came out second on the whole list of testers, accepting a promotion as engineer to Tower One in downtown Orlando. I kept that position for about four years, and auto extrication was an added responsibility from the beginning. The trade name for auto extrication/hydraulic rescue tools is "Jaws of Life." We were the first to arrive on the scenes of major automobile accidents, and we had to cut people free from seatbelts and bent steel using special cutters, spreaders, and extension rams. Downtown was the site of a significant number of accidents due to its close proximity to Disney World and all the other tourist attractions, and many out-of-state drivers were unfamiliar with our highways. The ghettos had their fair share of accidents as well, especially around the train tracks, and it wasn't unusual that these accidents often involved people's decisions to drive under the influence of alcohol or drugs. Ashley was still relying heavily upon me after Pops was gone, and I was dealing with several other family issues at any given time, so even when I was "off the clock," I wasn't always free to put my feet up and relax at home. This added to my constant lack of rest and increasing internal anxiety, even though I loved my sister and family dearly and responded to them as readily as I would anyone else in my life of constant emergencies.

A gorgeous fire department dispatcher, Mari Jo, had caught my attention in those days. I was lucky that she understood my hectic life, as she was in the same line of work, or else our relationship may have never taken off because my lifestyle did not afford me limitless afternoons for romantic picnics in the sunshine. (Lucky for me, our relationship *did* stand the test of time and stress, because that gorgeous dispatcher is now my wife and best friend.)

After another four years at Tower One, I began studying for the lieutenant's exam sometime in 1995. My station positions up to that point had taken so much out of me that I was then feeling the beginning stages of burnout, but I still saw the great need for dedicated responders, so instead of finding a new career, I decided to change the approach I took to my current one. Job fatigue was setting in fast, so it was crucial that I switch things up a bit as soon as possible.

Midway through my studies for the exam, I had dropped by my dad's barn to pick up a tool to work on my car. Dad kept a phone in the back of the barn, and I never answered it when it rang. I'm not sure what compelled me to do so on this particular occasion, but for some reason, when I heard the ringing that day, I took the call.

"Hello?"

"Is this Ed Taylor?"

"No, this is his son, Mark."

"Well, I'm calling from the Orlando Regional Medical Center. Hassie Taylor, Homer Taylor, Ida Taylor, and Clyde Taylor have all been involved in a car accident."

The man on the other end of the call was referring to my grandparents and my great aunt and uncle.

"Ida Taylor expired on the scene," he continued. "The other three are in critical condition in the intensive care unit right now, and we need someone to come down to identify the body. Is there any way you can come down to the hospital?"

As a trained responder, it was both my nature as well as my duty to not allow my shock or emotions to set in and keep me from efficient action. My worst nightmare during my days as a fireman was having to run a call on someone I knew, and this information may well have dropped me in my tracks and sent my head spinning, but I knew I had to keep my wits about me if I was going to give my family the support they needed at this moment. So I swallowed my shock and acted as immediately as I would have if this had been an anonymous station call.

On my way to the hospital, I dropped by my cousin's house and told him he needed to try to reach the family from his phone. Nobody carried cell phones in those days, I had no idea where my parents were, and my uncle and his family were at Disney World, so I had to have my cousin's help in getting the word out to all our other relatives. As soon as I had informed him of what was going on, I continued on to the hospital, determined to remain calm. I had only just ended a shift at work, so I still had my uniform on. I knew the operations of an emergency room, so I walked in, made a quick call to my then-girlfriend, Mari Jo, and then hurried through the ER-speak to carry me to the next task. The staff took me to my great Aunt Ida's body, and sure enough, it was her. The rest of the information given to me in my dad's barn was also confirmed by this point: my great uncle Clyde, grandmother Hassie, and grandfather Homer were all in critical condition in ICU after a young speedster had T-boned them on the highway.

For several hours, I remained there at the hospital with Mari Jo, who had raced to be there with me. But my time was not spent idly, as I ran from place to place assisting the medical team and seeing to all the needs of the ER crew between repeated attempts to get my parents on the phone. When I finally succeeded, they showed up right away. Later on, through the help of my cousin, more relatives eventually arrived.

Much tension tugged on my familial unit back then. Several people in my extended family didn't see eye to eye on anything, so, on top of the sadness and despair we were already dealing with, a couple of my relatives got into a knock-down, drag-out fight in the ER waiting room. Ashley was beside herself, everyone was fighting, Aunt Ida was gone, and my grandparents and great uncle were facing death. Plus, in the midst of all this tragedy, the issue of my upcoming lieutenant's exam was nagging at the back of my thoughts—and I wasn't remotely prepared to take that test. As much as I tried to distract myself with facts and figures to prepare for the test, my brain was just a bees' nest of buzzing chaos.

I remember praying, "Lord, I just can't do this. I've got a family to take care of. Only You know how I'm going to do on this exam. I've put everything I can into it. If it is Your will that I pass, then please give me the strength."

And then He did.

He must have known even better than I did how much I needed a change of pace.

Lo and behold, despite everything, I ended up coming out number two of the testers on that exam as well. Just after that, Uncle Clyde, who had flat-lined twice on the operating table in ICU, passed away during his subsequent care at a retirement home due to complications from the accident. Grandpa Homer had Alzheimer's before the wreck, so he was already heading downhill, and the tragedy put more strain on him than he could handle, so he passed away a short time later. Only Grandma Hassie survived the ordeal, and lived to be 102. (She passed away in 2017.)

With the grief of loss so recent in my heart and thoughts, I worked the way I always did, calmly and mechanically, taking my new promotion as lieutenant as seriously as any human could be expected to whilst trying to keep a positive attitude. Issues in Ashley's life mounted when she got married and quickly divorced. I spent a lot of time taking care of her whenever I could, because the relationship she had with my father was still not ideal, and we all knew she wouldn't instinctively turn to him. In the meantime, however, I knew the best experience I could get as a fire officer was through heavy submersion, so the best way I knew to sharpen my skills was to throw myself into the thick of it back at Station Two, our 12,000-call station. I worked that office for two years, but I never could shake that old burnout feeling. Eventually, I decided I couldn't take it anymore, and the twenty-five-year retirement was simply too far away for me to keep plowing ahead. Between the demands of my job, which is taxing enough in itself, and the family that needed me more and more every day, I knew I had met my limit. I had already made it a decade longer than many I had known who had already retired with Post-Traumatic Stress Disorder, so I was pushing myself beyond the healthy zone every hour that I remained in the service.

I made a plan to talk to my district chief the next time I saw him. When that conversation took place, I was relieved that he appreciated my position.

"Look," I said, "this is ridiculous. I've done my time here. I've got too much going on in my personal life, and I'm completely and totally burned out. I can't take it anymore."

"Alright, Mark. We'll put your float in."

I understood this gracious fire-service lingo very well. It meant that my name would be placed on a waiting list for another station, and as soon as there was an opening elsewhere, I would be repositioned for yet another change of pace. Hopefully then, my chief and I thought, I would be able to at least make it to my twenty-year mark for retirement benefits.

Before long, I was transferred to Station Ten, just outside Universal Studios. It would be my last station before retirement, but it ended up being even more intense than Station Two. The accidents there were even worse than in the downtown area. Tourist wrecks were prominent on the high-speed highways, and travelers weren't acquainted with our traffic. When they hit, they hit *hard*. We carried out as many as three auto extrications per day, dealing with a lot of trauma, and it was especially saddening when the vehicle was filled with families on vacation to meet Mickey Mouse: having to cut vacationing fathers, mothers, and children out of cars while they were bleeding, scared, and oftentimes unconscious. We had an amazing crew at Station Ten, however, so in regard to efficiency and chemistry on the job, it could have been far worse for both myself and the victims we tended to.

Life began to even out a lot for Ashley, so I used the last bit of free time I had to start my own business online. I had developed—or, rather, *the Lord* had developed through me as His servant to execute—the Special Operations Recovery Drag (SORD), a victim-extraction rescue device. When a downed victim or rescuer is incapacitated within a hot zone or danger zone, the only equipment available to us took between five to seven minutes on average to remove the victim from a ten-foot by ten-foot room, because of all the belts, buckles, snaps, and straps involved. If, during an emergency, a firefighter lost his grip on a piece of the equipment in a low-visibility state, he spent even more time frantically groping about blindly to find it. I found these extraction devices unacceptable in the crucial, time-sensitive scenarios I was used to in the service, so I drew up the specs on a new device and set out to order all the manufacturing materials and production services required to launch it. After what felt like ceaseless testing and field trials, the SORD was complete. I created a website with training videos and rescue images, and started contacting every rescue organization I could think of to promote it. The response I received was initially very encouraging, but I continued to face obstacles.

In addition to the SORD, I had also developed a line of rescue tools. That was the effort in my business that flopped before it got off the ground. Determined to keep all manufacturing within the U.S., after three years of searching, I signed a four-year contract with a U.S. manufacturing company. Because of the economy in the U.S. at the time and their inability to compete with Taiwan's pricing, the manufacture and sales of the tools never got off the ground. Then an ex-Delta Force military acquaintance who had some high-profile government connections decided to partner with me on the SORD. Our first Navy contract was for sixty-eight thousand SORD units, but something happened to the man who was positioned to represent the device to Navy leaders, and the deal fell through. Shortly thereafter, the senator of the Homeland Security Committee agreed to place an initial one hundred thousand SORD units in fire trucks all across the U.S., but he was thereafter caught in a scandal, and that deal also fell through.

My prayer following that update was, "Lord, I don't understand all of this. This was *Your* invention. It was never mine. What should I do?"

I had lost every lead, my partnership fizzled, my tools were a lost cause, the SORD now appeared to have been little more than an enormous waste of what little energy I had, and I couldn't bear the thought of continuing in the fire and rescue service. (I didn't know at the time that God's plan for the SORD was not over.)

Around this time, two years before I retired out of Station Ten, I started feeling my health decline.

Mentally.

Physically.

Emotionally.

I was going down, rapidly, into a pit from which I never saw myself emerging.

My life had begun a whole new—and debilitating—chapter...

chapter two

From Fighting Fires to Fighting for My Life

Mari Jo and I had enjoyed a little over five years as a married couple before this mysterious sickness crept in and changed everything. I hadn't advertised to her that her new life as a wife and mother of our "kids" (pets) would additionally be as a part-time nurse for me, because I hadn't known this was coming. Nevertheless, I gradually found myself depending on her help as symptoms of depression and fatigue increasingly consumed me with parallel waves of unbearable nausea, so I didn't hesitate to seek help.

One of the first doctors I went to see had known my family for a number of years. He was familiar with our family history and had a good reputation as not only a learned doctor but also an upright Christian man. I told him of my concern about PTSD, since I had seen so many other firemen retire with that disorder, but he felt it necessary to refrain from giving me such a diagnosis that early on.

"No, I do not want to do that to you, Mark," the doctor said genuinely. "I'm not going to label you right now. Let's just put you on Zoloft for about a month, and that should take care of it."

Zoloft is a drug used to treat PTSD, but it's also frequently administered for depression, panic disorders, OCD, and severe anxiety. I agreed to the treatment and it worked just like the doctor said it would, but the effects were not permanent. Not even close. Something was wrong with me that the doctor hadn't found. I enjoyed my grace period of floating on an external source of counterfeit, drug-induced peace for a while, but by the time another calendar year had passed, my symptoms returned full-swing.

I had never been so exhausted in my life, and it wasn't just a matter of sleep deprivation. Everything in me was letting go. I had always been a calm and collected person, willing to remain positive and keep facing each day with grit and determination, and the virtue of my occupation had always been its own reward when I saw another life saved as a result of my participation in the station's efficient response system. But something deep within me was breaking, and I was drowning in a pool of energy-sapping, emotional tar.

One memory sticks out to me as one of the earliest signs that I was giving up. I was lying in a cot in Station Ten between calls one night, staring at the ceiling. The sense of aimlessness I felt in that hour was thicker in the air of that room than any black smoke I'd been exposed to prior. Suffocating. Overpowering. Stifling. The drive I once had as a boy playing firetrucks with my neighbor pal had manifested into true passion as an adult, carrying me through what had been nineteen years of protecting and preserving human life, but all I could think of now was how meaningless it all appeared to be.

What am I doing here? I thought to myself. *I'm running myself day and night, over and over, killing myself slowly. I could be at home, in bed. I could be spending time with my wife. I could be playing with my animals. I could be living!*

The silence in the room toyed with me. Despite the absence of sound, "peace" was an oxymoronic concept. All I had ever wanted, my longest and dearest dream, was to be the third-generation firefighter that the Lord and Pops would both be proud of. One that stayed until the end. One that refused to be intimidated by any threat to mortality. One that could stand proud of reaching humanitarian goals and whose epitaph would reflect a life of committed provision for others. One whose ambition was anchored in the rock of my Creator. One who could always reach deep down and grasp ahold of the strength to press forward when morale waned.

But this… *This* I didn't see coming. Peace and steadfast determination were worlds away from me now.

I don't want to see anymore trauma. I've seen enough blood and fire. I have watched enough people die. I have been two minutes late too many times, and I'm weary of living with the images of brutal fatality in my mind. No more death!

I'm just…done.

Done.

Or perhaps I was *undone*. I couldn't tell. At the very least, the container that had been my drive to continue was now cracked, and the last remnants of resolve were leaking from within its vestiges.

I will never forget the state of mind I was in that day. It became the shift within me that marked the beginning of my internal deterioration.

The beginning of what almost killed me in the following decade.

In the back of my mind, however, one thought triggered an interesting contemplation that I would find myself clinging to for hope over and over again as the days worsened: *God must be allowing me to feel the weight of all this because He is calling me to another service—a Kingdom service.*

I would soon come to find out just how true that was.

I shared this thought with my chief.

"I'm leaving at twenty. I'm not staying for the twenty-five years, because I just feel that God is telling me to do something else."

"Is He calling you to preach?" he asked.

"No, I'm no preacher. I can't explain it. I just feel like He's calling me to do something else, and this is not it."

I'm glad I had such support and understanding from those above me back then. With or without their blessing, I had made my choice, but their understanding made my decision easier.

I had stored up about four months of vacation and sick-leave time, so in early September of 2005 I decided to spend it all back-to-back and rest early. I went in for my last shift on January 1, 2006, but I didn't tell anyone it was my last day until the last minute, because I didn't want anyone attempting to throw any parties or surround me with unwanted attention. I just wanted to make my exit and never look back. A few manly side-hugs and cavalier back-claps later, I was driving away from the station forever.

The next day, Mari Jo and I went to City Hall and met with the district fire chief to sign the retirement paperwork. Upon returning home, I wasted no time in officially severing myself from everything remotely connected to what was now the past. The second I walked over the threshold of our house, I set to work with my wife's help.

"Get a trash bag, Mari Jo," I hollered, making my way to the bedroom.

She didn't argue. She had seen everything I had been facing and understood better than anyone else how badly I needed to wake up the next day without ties to a life left behind. A moment later, she appeared in the doorway with a hefty, black plastic bag just in time for me to heap every uniform, T-shirt, badge, and boot from the service into it. Everything that said "Fire Department" had to go. Once my closet, drawers, and the rest of my belongings were cleared of all service gear, we heaped the entire load into the garbage can.

I still don't regret that decision to this day, even though it may have been an act carried out in part through impulse, because it became a cleansing from one life calling to another. I was only interested in looking one direction, and it wasn't backward. The paramount uncoupling between myself and firefighting that had taken place within me was sealed, and the disposal of my gear had been the only remaining symbolic act of this newfound devotion to whatever the Lord would give me next.

Just after my signal to the Lord that I was now His…He gave me a signal of His own.

On the evening of February 1, one month to the day from my last shift, I was asleep in bed. For whatever reason, Mari Jo had trouble sleeping that night and came to bed much later than usual. I heard her stirring around and climbing under the covers, and I opened my eyes to check the time. It was one o'clock in the morning. I asked her what she was doing up, and after she told me she hadn't been able to sleep, I rolled back over and closed my eyes.

What occurred next happened *immediately*.

Faster than the blink of an eye, I was caught up in a vision. It wasn't a dream, it wasn't a hallucination, and it wasn't my imagination. It was a reality that I could see and feel and experience on a plane of existence even more tangible than I had experienced during any season of earthly living. A vision of something so real and so important that it rendered all other human experiences from birth to death a mere prototype-encounter of life. What I saw will remain with me forever.

I was observing myself from above while my body was crouched in a kneeling position on the floor of the bedroom. The furniture was gone. My walls were the same cream color as they've always been, but my usually tan carpeting was now a deep, cobalt blue. I was speaking in tongues aloud. My right arm was extended out in front of my body, and I was writing on the floor with my index finger, which was illuminated from the inside out with a strange radiance like the glow of a candle's flame contained just under the skin. At certain moments, the light was bright enough that it traced upward into my hand. I couldn't see what I was writing, but as I followed the trail my finger was making in the fibers of this new, vibrantly colored carpet, I recognized the patterns of movement to be cursive.

Suddenly I was no longer above myself. I was viewing the floor from a first-person perspective. In front of me, a Presence appeared in the form of a thick, dark cloud, and I instantly knew that it was God. His magnificence at that moment defies all description here and now. No available patterns within the English language can bring explanation or justice to the awesomeness of that manifestation. He did not move, thunder, swirl about, or dissipate, nor did He utter a single audible order, but He remained there above and in front of me like a royal haze in the room, demanding by the very authority of His attendance that every knee bow and all mankind tremble. He was breathtakingly holy and formidable to the core. All-powerful. A Being whose supremacy, sovereignty, and dominion were so invincibly omnipotent that without even a movement or motion of any kind, one could be vaporized from existence at His mere thought-command…and I knew it.

A fear dawned within my soul so abundant and concentrated that no power in the universe—save God, Himself—could dilute it. It was not a fear that I was in danger, or that I was in the midst of any evil. It was a reverential fear, like a newly appointed servant lying prostrate in obeisant genuflection of a colossal governing force. Yet, a cowering pauper brought into the courtroom of the mightiest of earthly kings—one pauper so petrified that they soil their garments—would consider such an experience to be a cakewalk in comparison to this.

Although I didn't comprehend the depth of it at the time, I now know that I was in the presence of the fear of the Lord. And it was the most dominating thing I have ever felt to this day.

Out of my peripheral view on the left came another, smaller cloud that floated its way behind me and hovered firmly on my right side. Once this second presence maintained its position, I looked down at my hand. The glow from my fingertip continued, as did my cursive writing, and my mouth still articulated a language I'd never spoken before.

Then, just as suddenly as all this came to me, it all disappeared in an instant. I felt an odd sensation of my spirit traveling back into my body, awakening upon arrival as if my body and soul had been previously unraveled like a two-stranded cord and then twisted back together.

When I awoke, I found myself in a fetal position, curled into a ball. The fear remained with me to the point that I could not open my eyes. I had seen and experienced so many things in my life that would have turned stomachs or made a weak man shake, and as a fireman I had always had the ability to shut those feelings off in the line of duty. My survival instincts and my ability to face the unknown with bravery had always been strong. But at this moment, I was so afraid of what I might see that I laid there, still, recoiling from the room, eyes shut tight.

About fifteen minutes passed while I was in that state before I finally regained enough composure to take in my surroundings once more. The first thing I did was look toward the clock.

It was now 1:33 a.m.

I rolled over and woke my wife. I didn't hesitate to tell her of the details of the vision God had just handed me. As I spoke, she listened, and at the first opportunity she had to speak without interrupting me, she told me my voice was different. I thought of the veil that Moses had placed over his face in Exodus after it became radiant following his presence with God, and it made sense that, like Moses' face, my voice had changed after such a revelation. Deeper. Resonant. Like a clash between solemn shock and wonder on one end and the beginnings of understanding on the other.

Very little of this made sense to me, but I knew it was a message of inspired importance, so the following Sunday, I sought the counsel of a close friend of mine who happened to be a certified dream interpreter through John Paul Jackson's Streams Ministries International (a ministry dedicated to assisting hungry children of God in discerning His voice).

"Mark, you had a visitation from the Lord," my friend said. "The cloud in front of you was God. The smaller cloud standing on your right was an angel assigned to you. As you spoke in tongues, you were

29

speaking in mysteries, as the Bible says. The light coming from your hand is the anointing that God has given you for whatever it is you're going to write. The carpet, too, is significant, as it means you will affect both your own walk and the walks of others, and blue is the color of revelation. You wrote in cursive, because each person's cursive writing has a unique, personal flair, so even though the words that come out of you will be the Lord's, they will reflect your style of communication, just as the Holy Spirit impressed upon the writers of the Bible. You may not yet know what it was you were writing, but whatever it will be, you are now anointed to accomplish it."

I took my friend's words seriously, and ruminated upon them in the next several months. I would not discover until a great time had passed that God's decision to appear as a cloud was not at all unique to me. Moses described God in this way in Deuteronomy 4:11, the psalmist of 97:2 wrote of this phenomenon, and even the priests encountered it in the Holy Place in 1 Kings 8:10–12. The fact that God might appear as something other than light was, also, not unique, as He had appeared as a "horror of great darkness" upon Abraham in Genesis 15:12. Additionally, the cloud went ahead of the Israelites by day, leading them through the wilderness, and in that regard, God was also manifest as a cloud in order to provide direction.

The vision held much meaning that I had not unpacked in those first days, but I knew that God would clarify what He was calling me to do when the timing was right.

In the meantime, however, I had no idea how sick I had become. It's almost as if my body and subconscious mind had been working together in a mutual resistance against the wiles of this perplexing illness until I was able to cognitively comprehend I was now fully retired. Once that reality hit—once I began to grasp that it was really over and I wasn't going to be expected to show up for work and fight fires or respond to emergencies—my survival instincts collapsed and the sickness dawned upon me like a physical, emotional, mental disease.

Not six months after my retirement, I was naught but a shadow of the man I once was.

I couldn't eat. Nausea was a constant companion. My gut writhed at the mere mention of food. From esophagus to bowels, I was completely wrecked.

I couldn't move. Every muscle in my body, most of which had quickly begun to atrophy, was weakened to the point that I was quickly wasting away like an old man—weak, fragile, brittle, and slow—and at times my body shook from a lack of nutrients. Hot flashes crept through me from head to toe, making the room spin even worse than it did from the combination of hunger and nausea.

I couldn't sleep. Dark, terrible thoughts of loneliness and worthlessness consumed my once-rational consciousness, and every hour felt like an eternity. That terrible moment lying on the cot in Station Ten under the swells of meaninglessness had merely been a harbinger of my new existence—and now every day was just like that one had been...but worse, because there was no foreseeable end to this new form of internal consumption. I could not "retire" from this demoralizing cycle. I could not "put my float in" for a transfer away from the beast raging within my brain. There was no chief to whom I could say "enough is enough." So weakened was my body that I could not escape from the confinement of my bedroom for fresh air or fresh perspectives. I was a captive in the worst kind of prison, and my confinement had no release date, no "early out" for good behavior. Time moved so miserably slow that each tick of the clock sluggishly reverberated in my ears like a sadistic and taunting announcement that only a second had passed since the last sound.

Tick...tock.

Hours between each moment and the next.

Every trip to a new physician was critically painstaking. It was hard to remain optimistic as I received the same bewildering response over and over. Doctor after doctor. Nobody knew what was wrong with me. And because medical professionals couldn't locate the cause behind my regression, some of my family members started telling me it was all in my head. I was "imagining" my way into a withering, useless—and approaching catatonic—state of being.

This went on for months that stretched into the longest and most miserable years I've ever lived as I continued to deteriorate. My weight plummeted to about the same as it had been in high school. My clothing hung on my shrinking frame like limp rags. My old buddies from the fire stations still had lives as busy as mine used to be, so I didn't blame them that they never called anymore, but the sting of solitude was endless. Not that it mattered… I didn't have the strength to hold a phone up to my ear long enough to shoot the breeze anymore anyway.

But the absolute worst were those nights when I broke down and wept at the edge of the bed while my wife held me helplessly. I went from Mark Taylor—the calm and collected firefighter; the responder to all emergencies; the man who set the standard for emotional stability during the worst of all tragedies—to a fearful child. No one whom I had run calls with in my past would even recognize me then. I wanted my health back. I wanted my *life* back. I just wanted to be whole again. And though Mari Jo knew this, she was powerless to save me. I was lost. Irrefutably, unquestionably lost. (God bless Mari Jo for standing beside me through those horrible days…days I wouldn't wish upon my worst enemy.)

As time dragged on, like a proverbial sloth with supernatural powers over my every breath, my mother started caring for me in shifts when Mari Jo was at work. Years prior, Mari Jo had also left the fire department and was now working for the federal government. Mom and Dad had bought a two-story cabin on twenty acres, but they couldn't afford the entire lot of land, so in my healthier days they had halved the property, and my wife and I bought the half where we built our house. Our close proximity to my parents as next-door neighbors ended up becoming a huge blessing, because when my wife wasn't home, my mother could usually be there. It was a bit of a rollercoaster at the time, because I would go four or five days at a time without food, and then I would have a day or two when I could at least keep something down long enough to revive my strength to the point that I could walk from one room in my house to another without assistance. But these upswings never lasted long, and I always reverted to being bedridden for days in a row. On extremely rare occasions, I would have enough strength to walk to my Mom's and sit by the campfire, just me and the Lord, but the exertion of that outing would take its toll for weeks or months following.

There is no doubt in my mind: I was a dying man. A physician might argue that I had a long life ahead of me physiologically speaking, but if that was the quality of my life, I was as good as gone already. My will to live wouldn't have been what kept me going. For all intents and purposes, and from every desperate angle I could view from my own bleak perspective, I was dying. I felt as if it was only a matter of time until my already ailing body would catch up with my thoughts…and then death would be a welcome release.

At times, I found myself praying, "Lord, just take me home." But then I would think of my sweet wife. I would think of the family that still needed me. I would think of Ashley.

And I would think of the Lord's recent visitation and the subsequent ministry that implied.

Clearly, the Lord was with me, and He knew what He was doing in me while the Spirit worked to complete what He had started (Philippians 1:6). I just had to be patient and wait for all of this to make sense. Years later, I would repent for the moments I allowed my mind to entertain a death wish, but until a person has lived in such a constant state of decline, there is simply no describing the agony of it—especially when there are no answers, and therefore no treatment, because the illness was supposedly "all in my head." That diagnosis had been suggested so often that even I began to wonder if it might be true: Had I, in some fit of hysterics, caused all of this?

But I didn't have to question whether the spiritual undercurrents of my life were of my own doing.

In the months following that vision, I had many, *many* dreams of a spiritual nature. They didn't have that same living, breathing reality to them as the visitation from God had, and at that time I hadn't again felt my spirit re-lace into my body, but the dreams were clear in their imagery, and I was always able to recall the details the following day to search for meaning. I probably dreamed five or six dreams per night on average, and almost all of them occurred in that drifting state between wakefulness and sleep. Frequently, I saw myself interacting with angels. They looked like regular people, but they housed supernatural strengths and abilities that made them stand apart from normal man. I had been warned to test the spirits, even in dreams, so I made that the first order of business each time. "Who is Jesus Christ to you?" I would ask. If the angel remained silent or started to screech, scream, growl, and/or shake, I knew I was dealing with something dark, and I followed up with an immediate rebuke in Christ's name. If the angel's response was in great praise of Christ, and they found no difficulty or hesitation in voicing their layered adorations of how wonderful He was and all the works He had accomplished for the world, then I knew I was alright to go along with them and see what they were sent to show me.

Once, one of the angels picked me up and soared into the sky, above the earth's atmosphere, and straight into the stars. He pointed at a galaxy cluster and said, "Look, Mark. No man has ever seen this." After sending the description of that dream to a few master interpreters, we all understood it to mean that the Lord was increasing my discernment, and He was about to reveal things to me that no man had ever seen prior.

In another dream, the Lord, Jesus Christ, *Himself,* came to me and showed me a map.

"This is where the enemy and his legions are at right now. We're scrambling the enemy's radar as we speak," Christ told me.

By this time in my illness, I knew the Lord was calling me to a prophetic work sometime in my future if I ever recuperated, as so many people had come to confirm, so I began asking Him questions and voicing my concerns.

"Lord, I don't ever want to lead Your people astray. I just have a heavy heart about that, and I'm afraid I'm going to get it wrong when the time comes."

He met my eyes and said a single word: "Maturity."

"Am I going to see you again?" I asked, referring to my dreams.

"Maybe."

And each time I dreamed that I had walked or flown with the Lord or His angels, I slipped into sleep and awoke with a tingling electricity throughout my physical body. It wasn't a painful shock, nor was it unpleasant, like the prickling of a body part lacking circulation. It was a lovely sensation of transcendence that I found comforting.

But drifting into or out of sleep wasn't always a pleasant experience. There were certainly times when I found myself dreaming that I was in the presence of evil, and when that occurred, the experience was accompanied by something I soon began to call "waves." Instead of electricity, I felt a compression of swells, one after another, like rolling pins traveling up my skin in succession. When I felt this, I knew that the dream I was about to have or the one I was awakening from was not of God.

The first time this happened, just after Mari Jo had left for work at around five in the morning one day, my dog wanted to be let out, so I opened the door for her and went back to bed. Within a minute or two of allowing myself to relax, the bed behind me bent under the weight of something crawling up onto the mattress. My first thought was that it was my dog, but a split second after the waves began, I remembered I had let her outside. Then something started breathing on the back of my neck. I don't remember how I handled that specific incident, I only know that it was the first time I had such a real encounter with something demonic.

It would be years before I began to conscientiously differentiate between the electricity and the waves, but I did eventually come to sense the distinguishable patterns of both and know which were sent from the Lord and which were from the enemy. Afterward, I had many run-ins in dreams with spirits who didn't even try to hide their ill will against me. I would reach out and attack them back, always using the physical self-defense strategies I had learned to rely on as a fireman, and I could feel their bones under a thin, loose layer of skin. At one point it grew to two or three of these incidents per morning or night, and it was always whenever my wife wasn't around. Sometimes, they spoke to me. "I'm going to [expletive] you up," one had said before his attack. They were never successful, but really, neither was I. The attacks just kept coming, and for as many friends of mine that had knowledge in the arena of dream interpretation, none of them knew what this recurring visitation meant.

Part of the answer to this conundrum came when, in my dream-state, I finally decided I'd taken more than I could stand. I held out my fists to fight my attacker, determined that I was going to either take this thing down or die trying, and all of a sudden, a light shot through my stomach. I woke up so violently that I jerked in the bed and knocked my phone across the room. When I shared this with the master interpreters, they unanimously agreed that "the Lord is encouraging you to find a different way of warfare." I had simply spent too many years battling unwanted aggression like a street fighter. I was relying too much on my own abilities, and God was letting me know that it was time to shift into relying on His.

All of this, I would come to find out, was my training for the call. And although the attacks were nowhere near over, I would remember this lesson of light in the days to come…especially when the enemy began to silence my voice.

All of this was also taxing me beyond my wildest dreams while my mind and body continued down a trail of mystery disease… Just when I thought I couldn't live like this anymore, I received a life-changing phone call from Ashley.

I can't begin to tell you the relief that came during my first appointment with Dr. Vanlue, another Christian doctor who cared deeply about his patients. My sister had gone to see him and he came highly recommended by her, so I sought his professional assistance, figuring I had nothing to lose. Before he even met with me, he ordered blood work. About three weeks later, when the results were in, I went to see him. Having never met the man in my life, I was surprised when his analysis came so quickly. After shaking his hand and seating myself at his desk, he looked at me with his nurse standing nearby and launched straight into it.

"Mark, this is *not* in your head."

I was stunned... Speechless! Could he have some list of real answers for me?!

"Every bit of this is physiological. You have a lot going on here."

With what little strength I had left, I leaned farther into my seat and forced my ears to open and the cogwheels of my mind to turn in order to fully receive the golden gift of elucidation he was about to give.

"You have an extremely low thyroid, you have *severe* adrenal burnout from running day and night with the fire department, and you have the hormones of a seventy-year-old. If you take any one of the numbers that I'm seeing here in your blood work and compare them to what the charts say is normal, it answers why a patient would be suffering from serious anxiety and depression. But if you link *all of these three together*, and with numbers like yours, I don't even know how you're getting out of bed."

At that, his nurse nodded and reaffirmed it with the same words. "I don't know how you're getting out of bed, either."

"I'm not, most of the time," I said.

"I can see why," she answered, eyes wide. "This is unreal!"

"How you're even talking to me right now," Dr. Vanlue continued, waving his arms in the air for emphasis, "is beyond me. You should be in a hospital bed right now. In my thirty years of practice, I've never seen a thyroid this low. Ever."

We continued to discuss what all the numbers meant, what they were supposed to be, and the treatment options for regulating them. I left his office with a boost in morale and headed for home grateful. I was no longer a victim of the mystery disease of "my own head's" creation. I was now receiving the help I had needed for years since my retirement. I still thank the Lord for His leading me to Dr. Vanlue.

chapter three

A Divine Appointment

Now that I had the beginning to my answers, I knew I was responsible for more than just relying on one man's rehabilitation program. As soon as I found the energy, I headed over to Tampa, Florida, to visit a ministry there called Inner Healing so I could work on cleansing my mind while Dr. Vanlue worked on restabilizing my body. The beginning of that treatment required a weekly visit for the first four weeks, followed by intermittent maintenance visits after that. Inner Healing focused on internal forgiveness and repentance toward restoration of the soul, which, for me, resulted in an adjustment of my worldviews and perspectives. I wanted to be a clean vessel for the Lord to use the way He wanted, so I had to heal from the habits of depression and anxiety. For twenty years, I had been on the streets professionally, but my entire life I had only known one kind of battle, and it was not the Lord's. I knew very well that God had told me to put my fists down and move into His brand of warfare, so now that I had a doctor slowly bringing my thyroidal, adrenal, and hormonal numbers closer to where they ought to be, I used the resulting gusto to diligently pursue rehabilitation of my spirit.

Another symptom that I was well aware of also needed to be treated: As a fireman, I had to click into survival mode and build up a wall around my emotions and concepts of human mortality. I saw death and injury so often, and my role was always to react calmly by using rescue protocol. In doing so, however, over time, my ability to value or treasure the lives of others also became a professional endeavor—a detachment, of sorts, through a constant fight-or-flight psychology that went along with the job of saving lives. And although I cared deeply for people (I would not have been in that line of work if I hadn't), death was so close to home that I had lost a crucial connection to humanity as I repeatedly disengaged in the line of duty. So the Lord was working on me through Inner Healing Ministries as well as Dr. Vanlue's treatments to break down those walls and reestablish my natural concern for the value of people.

Progress was slow but steady, and I wouldn't reach full functionality in life for almost eleven years after I retired. Since balancing the thyroid relies on the existent stability of the adrenal gland and hormones—and vice versa—simply taking a pill does not make it better. Recovery involves a lengthy and strenuous process of slowly bringing all numbers into sync with the others. As such, although I was getting help, I was still terribly sick most of the time. Yet, while I awaited the day I could acknowledge my normality and move on to the next step in life, I was still experiencing spiritual dreams every night, many with good messages from the Lord or His angels, and many others with threats from the enemy.

One night when I was feeling particularly down, I dreamed that the Holy Spirit placed His hands on the back of my shoulders in a gentle and comforting massage. Butterflies were fluttering all about the room, which I discovered later was a sign of transformation. The Spirit's voice whispered in my ear two words I had never heard: "Shakina Kami." I took this information to my interpreter friend; he told me they were names, and then gave me a resource to look up their meaning. "Shakina" as a name is African in origin, and it translates "Beautiful One." "Kami" is an Indian name, and it translates "Whose Desires Are Fulfilled." Additionally, both of these names, once traced back to some of their etymological roots, point to some renderings in Hebrew and Japanese that ring true to my spirit to this day. *Shechinah* in Hebrew means "settling" or "dwelling," and it was most commonly used in reference to the dwelling of the divine presence of the Lord in one's home or life. *Kami* is Japanese for "God" or "Lord," and was therefore used by Japanese converts to Christianity and Protestant missionaries circa 1600 to refer to Christ—and, by extension, to the provision of the Lord of Hosts over one's life. It is also a derivative of the Japanese compound word *kamikaze*, the "divine wind of God" or the "divine wind of God's providence" (*kami*, "God"; *kazi*, "divine wind"; used in this manner for ages before it became known as the "suicide flyer" of World War II).

I was floored when I realized that the Creator of the universe had renamed me as He had the patriarchs in the Old Testament, but I was even more amazed when I began to digest the translation of the new name. In the simple "Shakina Kami" sound the Holy Spirit uttered was the following: "Beautiful One Whose Desires Are Fulfilled, and in Whose Life the Lord Dwells with the Divine Wind of Providence." Not only was He calling me beautiful, despite all my recent trudging through the mud of despair and depravity, but He was also telling me that the desires of my heart were His, and that they would be fulfilled through the direction of His all-knowing and divine wind.

Add this to the butterflies that sweetly and gently dipped here and there all over the room during that dream, and the meaning is clear: I was no longer the man I was...I was being transformed into this new identity. I was no longer simply Mark Taylor...

I was Shakina Kami.

And I would live up to that name to the best of my abilities from that day forward, willing at any moment to receive the orders the Lord handed me, and willing at all times to continue maturing into this identity as the Lord had told me to do in the dream with the map of the enemy.

I had no way of knowing that His first requirement of me for the Kingdom was just around the corner.

In 2011, during my early stages of treatment with Dr. Vanlue, I had been watching Fox News as a distraction from my nausea and anxiety. Donald Trump was on the air talking about his ideas of international currency policies, but he had not yet announced that he would be running for president. I didn't have any grand opinions or concepts about Trump. I had seen him on the news before, and I had heard him discuss politics, but I can't say I ever really paid close attention or considered him more of an answer to our nation's troubles than any other potential candidate. He was just another guy with his own impressions of how things should be handled. Without officially having announced his intention to run at this point, his was one name among thousands of others who voiced their convictions on the airwaves when given the platform.

My body and mind were exhausted, as they usually were in those days, and I was only taking in every third word or so of what Trump was saying. Because of this, I know what happened next did not come as a result of being inspired by his speech, because to this day I can't even recall what his official position was at that time on the subject of currencies. It wasn't by the inspiration of man, but by the inspiration of God that my spirit tingled with anticipation.

From out of the blue, I started to discern an odd sensation of certainty, as if I were about to be told something that had already been solidly ordained in the spiritual realm. It was more than a mere "sensing" of incoming revelation—it was a "knowing."

I stood to my feet. My eyes saw the screen and my ears were beginning to tune in a little more to what Trump was saying, but my mind and heart were preparing to be the true recipients of whatever I was going to learn. It never had anything to do with Trump's words, but something about hearing his voice at this moment popped out as a different experience from all other times I had heard him speak.

And then, like a ringing in my spiritual ears, came the Lord's disclosure.

You are hearing the voice of a president.

I knew all at once that the vision I'd had of me on my bedroom floor speaking in tongues and writing in cursive on the carpet was demanding me to take action. I could not deny that the Lord had been clear when He used the vision that night to warn me that there would be a day when I would write a message that would affect my walk and the walk of others. What rang true in my spirit in that instant was that *this* was the day, and *this* was the message. I was hearing the voice of a future United States president, and the Holy Spirit had an enormous word for all who had ears to hear.

It wasn't a trance. My body wasn't "taken over" by anything or anyone. The ceiling of my house didn't split apart, there were no trumpets, and there were no supernatural manifestations in the corporeal world. But I knew it was time to pick up my pen and obey the directive the Lord had given me. So I made my way to my office, sat down, and began to write. With each word, I prayed that the Holy Spirit would guide me to write what He wanted me to say, and *only* what He wanted me to say. I didn't want my own person to be in the words in any way. This message was not Mark Taylor's to give. This message did not belong to Shakina Kami. This word was from the Lord, and I was resolute in keeping my own thoughts, opinions, and concepts far away from it.

In the same way that the string of words had hit me in the living room telling me I was "hearing the voice of a president," as I kept my pen moving, more words were forming into complete sentences, and I wrote with confidence as the Lord led:

The Spirit of God says: I have chosen this man, Donald Trump, for such a time as this. For as Benjamin Netanyahu is to Israel, so shall this man be to the United States of America! For I will use this man to bring honor, respect, and restoration to America. America will be respected once again as the most powerful and prosperous nation on earth (other than Israel). The dollar will be the strongest it has ever been in the history of the United States, and will once again be the currency by which all others are judged.

The Spirit of God says: The enemy will quake and shake and fear this man I have anointed. They will even quake and shake when he announces he is running for president; it will be like the shot heard across the world. The enemy will say, "What shall we do now? This man knows all our tricks and schemes. We have been robbing America for decades; what shall we do to stop this?" The Spirit says: HA! No one shall stop this that I have started! For the enemy has stolen from America for decades and it stops now! For I will use this man to reap the harvest that the United States has sown for and plunder from the enemy what he has stolen and return it seven-fold back to the United States. The enemy will say, "Israel, Israel, what about Israel? For Israel will be protected by America once again." The Spirit says: Yes! America will once again stand hand and hand with Israel, and the two shall be as one. For the ties between Israel and America will be stronger than ever, and Israel will flourish like never before.

The Spirit of God says: I will protect America and Israel, for this next president will be a man of his word; when he speaks the world will listen and know that there is something greater in him than all the others before him. This man's word is his bond and the world and America will know this and the enemy will fear this, for this man will be fearless. The Spirit says: When the financial harvest begins, so shall it parallel in the spiritual for America.

The Spirit of God says: In this next election they will spend billions to keep this president in; it will be like flushing their money down the toilet. Let them waste their money, for it comes from and it is being used by evil forces at work, but they will not succeed, for this next election will be a clean sweep for the man I have chosen. They (the enemy) will say things about this man, but it will not affect him, and they shall say it rolls off of him like the duck, for as the feathers of a duck protect it, so shall my feathers protect this next president. Even mainstream news media will be captivated by this man and the abilities that I have gifted him with, and they will even begin to agree with him: says the Spirit of God.

This was a prophecy that would change everything for everyone from one border of the country to the other. A prophecy that would alter the course of history for the globe.

This did not happen because *I* was great. It happened because *He is*, and He can use any willing person for His purposes…even a retired firefighter with zero college education and a frail body.

After I had penned the "Commander-in-Chief Prophecy" regarding Trump, I didn't know what to do with it, because I was so used to being cooped up at home that I didn't have many contacts to share it with. So I set it aside, fully believing that one day it would become clear to me whose hands it should be placed in. I did casually give a copy of it to Dr. Vanlue and a buddy of mine named Brian Phillips, as well as my family, but this early on, that was about all.

It was around this time that a major wave of nonphysical healing would happen in my life, though it wasn't without its own brand of struggle.

Something about the enemy's attacks upon me several times per morning as I was waking from my sleep was ringing a warning that a door had been left wide open somewhere for demonic oppression. I had sought inner healing, I had prayed both alone and with great spiritual leaders, and I had gained the counsel of numerous reputable dream interpreters and theologians…but the attacks just kept on. I went from person to person looking for help, but nobody had the answers. Everything I could be doing on my end, including pleading the blood of Jesus over everything in my life and calling upon His name while I was awake, was my standard practice. And although I definitely saw the declination of oppressive activity, it was always there, tormenting me even on a smaller scale. Ever since the dream I'd had when the Lord told me to drop my fists and enter His brand of warfare, I had made daily attempts to fight against these dark visitations in another way, but in these dreams, conflicts still turned physical between myself and the demonic aggressor in self-defense, because I couldn't seem to call out in my sleep. It was like those dreams wherein people try to call for help and they open their mouths and nothing comes out. It became clear in a short time that the very thing the dark entities wanted to do was squelch my voice and assault me—provoking me to fight back with the same clenched fists the Lord had told me to ignore—and deliver me into a state of distraction and chaos.

Eventually, I got in touch with an intercessor named Melissa through a generational deliverance ministry stationed in California. Melissa explained that although we can cleanse our own personal sins through prayer, it does not cleanse the sins that have been committed before us in our familial lineage (Exodus 20:5; 34:7; Numbers 14:18; Deuteronomy 5:9). So we tackled generational deliverance from every angle, addressing and praying over everything we could think of, from idolatry to addiction to perversion and beyond—but like an onion, we kept pulling back a layer to find nothing underneath but the next layer. One by one, we ruled out each potential cause of affliction in my ancestry…until Freemasonry came into discussion.

When that one came up, we hit a wall, and we knew we needed extra help.

Many of the practices surrounding Freemason vows, pledges, and duties involve pronouncing curses on one's self and his or her descendants that cause horrifying things to happen if that person should fail in any duties or promises. There is no way of knowing what may have been the exact goings-on in the Taylor line or any individual ancestor's involvement in Freemasonry, but from what I was now hearing, the description fit. Someone in my heritage somewhere had pronounced a Masonic curse to befall on us, and it was now affecting me. I certainly don't immediately place the fault of it all on those in my current family who are Freemasons, but historically, we have had many in the family (several of which were high up on the rungs of leadership), and several are alive and active today, including my uncle.

Melissa told me of another intercessor, Sarah, who could be available for a future session consisting of the three of us together, and I agreed. We set up a telephone conference call to take place soon after, and I told my mother to pray as well.

When the scheduled day arrived, I sat in my office preparing for the session. The weather was sunny and clear outside, not a cloud in the sky anywhere, no heatwaves, no sprinklings, no wind, no extreme dryness or humidity, no sign whatsoever of anything out of the ordinary on an otherwise perfectly bright summer day. But five minutes before the phone rang, lightning struck between my house and my parents' house. It wasn't followed by any rain, thunder, or clouds. It wasn't accompanied by anything at all. It was simply a solitary, powerful strike of lightning at random in the middle of the day, and it was so loud and booming that it shook both houses with a great, rapid-earthquake vibration. Mom and Dad also heard and felt its intimidating reverberation.

I received it as a sign from the Lord that He was going to strike down my enemies through the fervent prayer of the intercessory phone call.

Once the session began, the three of us prayed diligently, without ceasing, for several hours. We asked the Lord for divine guidance, wisdom, and deliverance from all strongholds against me and my family. On and on we prayed, our minds and hearts set to continue for as long as it took. A few dramatic moments transpired unexpectedly, one of

47

which was quite shocking. Sarah told me that an image had appeared suddenly in her mind. A man in a goat mask was conducting a mock Masonry ritual, using me as the sacrifice. He spoke in a strange language as he moved about and uttered my name intermittently.

We knew then that we had found the snare. And we went after it.

Our determination to keep praying could have carried us into a week-long ordeal for all we knew, but we were dedicated toward change. Luckily for us, after about the third hour, something suddenly lifted. We all felt it. It was like the veil was torn back and a sensation in the air alerted us to new freedom. A release had fallen upon me. A peace wrapped around each of us praying in different locations of the country. Whatever this strange occurrence was that had been carried out against my name had been defeated.

Confirmation came the following morning.

"You're never going to believe what happened," my mother said as I stepped up onto her porch for a visit. She had been informed about the call between Melissa, Sarah, and me, and she also took the lightning strike to be a sign from God.

"What's that?"

"Your daddy was on the phone with his brother this morning," she stated, referring to my Mason uncle. "He was really angry, and when your dad asked him why, he said, 'Because my wife lost her ring, and I lost my Mason ring.'"

"Why in the world would Dad's brother call to tell him that?" I wondered aloud. It wasn't the kind of conversation they would normally have, and the subject seemed to have come up out of nowhere. Yet the significance of it was not left vacant.

The rings of a husband and wife represent a covenant. My uncle's ring was Masonic. The loss of both in one day—the very day following the intercession—represented to me a breaking of the Masonic and covenantal curse that someone had placed on me.

I knew it was over then.

And it was.

The attacks stopped immediately. Gone completely. Not another crazy, voice-silencing dream or visitation from the enemy ever bothered me again…that is, *until* my "Commander-in-Chief Prophecy" went public and my name began to appear in the media circus all across the states…

The prophecy I had written in 2011 did not come true in 2012 like I thought it would. President Barack Obama won a second term, so I thought for a while I had gotten it all wrong. Nevertheless, I truly believed that the Holy Spirit had guided me that day, so I continued to believe the message had some kind of relevance to God's people in some way, even if it wasn't what I would have thought.

Because of the most recent round of spiritual healing, when a stronghold over my life had been loosed for good, gusto and determination revived within me, and I had a newfound interest in seeing what God *really* had to say about Donald Trump, regardless of what the last election showed. Here and there, whenever I thought it appropriate, I shared the prophecy with people I felt had similar convictions about the nation as my own. I was surprised when some of my acquaintances took the "Commander-In-Chief Prophecy" very seriously, sharing with me that they believed what I had written was without a doubt a message from the Lord. My confidence grew the more others recognized that what I had written was beyond my own imagination. Before long, near-complete strangers were getting their hands on the prophecy and reassuring me that they, too, heard God's voice lifting off the page. So, when I shared some doubts with a few of them about the timing—noting that the prophecy had been written on April 28, 2011, and then Obama won a second term—they didn't hesitate to remind me that Trump hadn't even announced he was running at that time. In the same way that Trump hadn't "lost," because he hadn't decided to run for president yet, my prophecy wasn't "wrong" like I thought it might have been just because Trump hadn't jumped in the running and stole the win from Obama in 2012.

The next step in the process, then, was waiting to see if Trump would run in 2016.

And then, a few weeks after I had started to open up about the prophecy, Trump's plans to win the presidential election in 2016 was all over the news...

Some within my growing support group sprang to life, supportively helping me get this prophetic word out there to everyone possible. God placed me uncountable times in just the right place on just the right day and in just the right hour to make unbelievable connections, and overnight, the "Commander-In-Chief Prophecy" was falling into the hands of major media moguls all around the U.S., some of whom were heavily involved in Christian television. As word reached me of their reactions, it was becoming obvious that God was using this prophetic document to speak to each of them in a similar way, as their responses were equally supportive.

I could hardly believe the momentum this movement had gained so quickly!

Here I was, a retired fireman with no college degree, and nothing particularly charismatic about my somewhat reclusive personality, and people were materializing from out of the woodworks, all over the country, to add their connections and skillsets to the work of seeing Donald Trump in office. Then again, it wasn't about *me*, and it never had been. It couldn't have been, because from the beginning I was never enormously popular, I had hardly any contact with the outside world since my body had weakened, and the prophecy I had penned was written years prior about a man *nobody* would have seen as a national leader at the time.

It all seemed...well, *crazy* to say the least.

There was no doubt in my mind that the attention the prophecy gained was not upon *me*, but upon the Lord. And now, people were working around the clock on the Lord's behalf to see His chosen leader win the office.

As history does tell, the "Commander-In-Chief Prophecy" inspired the launching of a national prayer chain that took place over the phone in the morning each day, and it was accessible by anyone in the world who wanted to dial in at the scheduled time. The prayers were led by some extremely prominent ministers, among which were:

- Evangelist Billye Brim
- Evangelists Richard and Lindsay Roberts
- Evangelists Harry and Cheryl Salem
- Pastors Gary and Drenda Keesee
- Pastor Lynn Braco
- Pastor Mike Atkins
- Pastor Dana Gammill
- Pastors Michael and Maria Durso
- Evangelists Bob and Audrey Meisner
- Chaplains Keith and Judith Hemila
- Evangelist D. J. Daly
- Intercessor Melissa Leggett
- Pastor Dave Williams
- Pastors George and Terri Pearson
- Pastor Sharon Daugherty
- Worship leaders and Bible teachers Stephen and Pam Marshall
- Pastor Tony Cooke
- Pastors Jacque and Tina Jacobs
- Evangelist and Bible teacher Dutch Sheets
- Watchmen Broadcasting station owner and Bible teacher Dorothy Spaulding
- Pastor Mark Barclay
- Pastor and evangelist Kenneth Copeland
- Pastor Keith Moore
- Pastors Ronald and Patricia Merthie
- Pastor and evangelist Judy Jacobs
- Intercessor Suzanne Hinn

- Pastor Bob Rodgers
- Pastors Mel and Desiree Ayres
- Pastor Joe Manno
- Pastors Paul and Marcia Santos
- Evangelist Leigh Valentine
- Pastor Ron Johnson
- Pastor Rick Joyner
- Pastor Andrew Wommack
- Pastor Robb Thompson
- Businessman and former NFL football player D. J. Dozier
- Promptness' Cheryl Strika
- Pastor Marion Farrar
- Evangelist Dorthe Lee
- Pastor Ray Hadjstylianos
- Businessman and Charisma Magazine owner Steve Strang
- Pastor Eddy Paul
- Pastor Theo Wolmarans
- Pastor and evangelist Karen Wheaton
- Pastor David Crack
- Pastor Keith Butler
- Pastor and prophet Hank Kunneman
- Evangelist Michael Koulianos
- Bible teacher and Cornerstone Television CEO Don Black
- Bible teachers and The Jim Bakker Show hosts Jim and Lorie Bakker
- Businessman and author Steven Scott
- Pastor Paul Goulet
- Pastor and Bible teacher Larry Huch

The prayer chain also featured guest appearances from musicians Stephen and Pam Marshall, as well as Rusty Meredith, who sang "That's the America I Love" by Jeanne Dukes.

America lit up the phone lines every day at the same time. It was incredible. Everybody who was anybody in the Christian world was spreading the word: "Call in and pray with us!" So intense was the response that when the hotline company could no longer accommodate the number of callers, the people had to cluster together and listen over the speakerphone in groups. These same groups would then remember their shared experience and pray together, and before I could blink, the whole nation was on fire in prayer every day for the Lord to have His will in our country's future.

On several occasions, one of the prayer chain guests prayed for a miracle, and the miracles would happen that same day. For instance, Karen Wheaton once prayed, "Father expose the hidden lies in Jesus' name," and before that very hour was over, the news exploded with updates regarding the lies that had been hidden in Hillary Clinton's emails. One after another, "mysterious" (translation: divinely guided) trigger events like this continued to take place until Trump's run for the presidential seat didn't look quite as impossible to the whole world as it had only weeks prior.

Every day from the start of the prayer line to Election Day, my life, and the lives of every believer that I knew, was consumed in prayer. We already knew in advance that Trump would be the winner of the November 8, 2016 race—because God had made it clear in no uncertain terms who His chosen Commander was—but we also knew that God blesses those who seek His face and His will in everything, so we prayed ever fervently that He be in the ultimate control tower. As one enemy of Trumps after another fell during the campaigns, our faith was strengthened.

Then, just moments after the election booths opened on that fateful day, contributors of the national prayer line participated in an organized blowing of the shofar all across the country...and when the United States turned red on every news screen across the globe, we were thrilled...

But we weren't surprised.

It was what He said He would do from the beginning.

And it was *not* God's last message on the matter.

PART TWO

The Message

The Election Was Only the Beginning

Before Donald Trump swept the nation with the words "Make America Great Again," a slogan registered for his campaign in July of 2015, God had already told me that He would bring greatness to us again. He told me that He had chosen Trump as His anointed, *for such a time as this.*

His phrase wasn't necessarily a new one. Previous generations of politicians had referenced "greatness" as an attribute that America was losing, its restoration a worthy endeavor that they would make promises about striving for. Many campaign assurances over the years by countless would-be leaders alluded to their abilities to "reinstate greatness" within our country. So why was it so revolutionary this time around?

Because this time, *God* had chosen the words. *God* had chosen the man. *God* was putting the words onto the chosen man's lips, and He was giving the people ears to hear.

For such a time as this...

The prophecy became a part of a political frenzy and a prayer movement that caught on, rocking the nation and dramatically changing its direction, and, for the first time in a very long time, it caused people to have hope.

But it doesn't end there. There's more that the Lord has said to me—more that He has to say to you, if you will only hear the message.

It is time for the Church to bend our knees, fold our hands in prayer, turn our eyes upward, open our ears, and hear the word of the Lord.

> *If my people, which are called by my name,*
> *shall humble themselves, and pray, and seek my face,*
> *and turn from their wicked ways, then will I hear from heaven,*
> *and will forgive their sin, and will heal their land.*
>
> 2 CHRONICLES 7:14

The prayer movement and the vocal, grassroots momentum of this country were undeniable appointments during the election of 2016. Trump's victory was irrefutable proof that people are ready to see change. And I don't mean the kind of change that Obama promised during his campaign, either. I mean real, deep-down, gut-level changes that can only happen when the people unite, hear the voice of God, and take action to bring about a real difference from what they have allowed themselves to settle for. This is the kind of change that can only happen when people are willing to stand up, leave their comfort zones, share the Gospel, and pray—with no alternate agenda—for *real* transformation from the ground up. When this happens, a nation's leadership can change from the top down.

Many people think that because Trump won the election, the war was won. This couldn't be farther from the truth. A battle has been won, to be sure, and we can be thankful for the triumph. But the Church still has other goals it needs to meet. Regarding *only this accomplishment,* God had told me that we needed to be steady in prayer about three objectives pertaining to the election of 2016 and its aftermath:

- Donald Trump needed to be elected. God has anointed him for such a time as this.
- Donald Trump needed to be inaugurated.
- After these previous two objectives were met, God would begin to purge the land. During this time, the Church would be required to transform, rise to the occasion, and take ground. When ground is taken, the Church is to hold it at all costs.

We are not done yet. The first two of these objectives have been accomplished now as I write this. But the third, and possibly the most important, is yet to come. The land will be purged. The Church's response is vital at this time. The Army of God, the Body of Christ, *must* stand tall and lead the way during this groundbreaking moment. I have more to share with you. God did not just use me to pass along a message about a guy who needed to be elected president. This is only one battle victory, and the war is yet to be won. Onward Christian soldiers! We must unite and await our orders from our Supreme Commander, God. There is more He, also, has to say to you.

He that hath ears to hear, let him hear.
MATTHEW 11:15

Before we go any farther, I will be candid and tell you that I am aware there are those who doubt me—be it my sincerity, the authenticity of my messages, or the source of the information that I receive. I have been mocked on YouTube and Facebook, become the brunt of jokes, and have even withstood threats for my disclosures and writings. I have been called a false prophet, a liar, you name it—as well as being told that I needed to repent or I would be thrown into the lake of fire. In some ways, I have been surprised by all of this. I mean, I knew the Church was in bad shape, but the Lord really pulled the veil back and showed me a vision of the Church I had never seen before. This experience has shown me how far many believers are from the voice of God.

In response, I will tell you that when God gives a word to one of His followers, it is common for that person to suffer persecution.

And he said, Verily I say unto you,
no prophet is accepted in his own country.
LUKE 4:24

But Jesus said unto them, A prophet is not without honour,
but in his own country, and among his own kin,
and in his own house.
MARK 6:4

Many have asked where I get the nerve to call myself a prophet. They question where I got the qualification. The funny thing is, I do not call myself a prophet. Although I feel that my calling is to be a seer or to prophesy, I don't actually call myself a *prophet*. I feel like that title carries with it a certain place of honor, and I have a long way to go before feeling worthy of such a claim. I am just a regular man who follows the Lord's prompting, someone who is at times given information that I am required to share. It is an honor and a duty to be used by God in this way.

I don't consider myself an educated person at all. I don't have a degree in anything, I've never been to seminary, and I've never been to Bible college. I am just an ordinary, common guy—an everyday person who has yielded himself to the Lord Jesus to be used in whatever capacity He chooses. It's important for me to encourage people with this central truth: It doesn't matter where you're at. God can and will use you right where you are.

When I first began to receive words from the Lord, my two biggest concerns were about accuracy and responsibility. I didn't want the restricted capacity of the flesh to interfere with the message that God would channel through me. I prayed that the communications I pass along from God would be completely spot-on, keeping with *precisely* what the Lord was telling me would never lead anyone astray. Because of this, I test the spirits when I am visited, and I shroud all my writings in prayer. Some of them take weeks to write, because I am immersing them in prayer as I meditate on them. Jesus told me during one of the visitations that with maturity comes the accuracy and authenticity that I pray for daily. I strive always to measure up to the calling to which God Himself has chosen me.

When I know that God is giving me a word, it rarely comes all at once. It often starts in the core of my being as a small, agitated stir that builds over time. This phase can sometimes take weeks. I respond by beseeching the Lord's leading and continue to prayerfully consider the message I am pondering until the Holy Spirit tells me to write. As I'm writing, I listen for God's voice and ask Him to direct my pen. I allow Him to use me as a conduit for the message He is delivering, until He has conveyed everything He wants said. When it is written, I make no further changes to it. I deliver it as it is written by the hand of God through my own.

I will tell you this: Man qualifies the *called*. God qualifies the *chosen*.

I never asked for this. I was sick to the point of near death in my bed when the visitations began. Some visits were so frightening that I would not wish them on anybody. Prophesying, by its very nature, places a person under attack. Critics come out of the woodwork, looking for ways to exploit any weaknesses. Any positive exposure a person in this situation gets is matched, at least, by negative publicity and reproach. This was not something solicited, studied for, chased after, or achieved on some sort of success ladder. God has chosen me to be a mere messenger. I am just a vessel.

Why did God select me to deliver these messages? I don't know. But if you yield to God, He will use you also. It doesn't matter who you are, what your background looks like, your financial status, educational experience, or current situation, if you surrender to His will and place yourself in His loving hands, God can and absolutely *will* use you.

So what is God saying to you? What is God saying to the Church? He has so much to disclose to all of us if we'll only submit our hearts and listen. For each one of us is a part of all this, and you, yourself, are not here by coincidence nor accident.

You exist here and now, as part of His plan.

For such a time as this...

chapter four

The Modern-Day D-Day

God speaks to everyone in imagery that they can understand. In the Bible, He often uses horses to illustrate what will come next. Many believed that the American thoroughbred racehorse, Secretariat, was a prophetic sign to the Church because of his miraculous accomplishments. On the evening of July 24, 2011, while I was sitting in my living room watching the movie *The Secretariat* with my wife, I heard the Lord say, "There's another one coming." Although the words were not audible, He said it distinctly, more than once. I immediately went to my office and started writing down what the Holy Spirit was telling me. When I was finished writing, I had penned the following prophecy, entitled "The Great Horse":

> The Spirit of God says, "There's another one coming, there's another one coming! It's a horse! That's right, a horse!"
>
> The Spirit of God says, "There's another one coming, a horse, a great champion, that I have created, greater than the champions before him, for the champions before him were great, but this one will be greater. For as the great champion

Secretariat was great and his record never broken, this one that is coming will shatter all records before him. For as the Secretariat was a prophetic sign for the Church in that generation, so shall this horse be for this generation. For this horse shall be a sign to my Church for the time they are in. He will also represent my Church in the spirit realm. They will run and not get tired; they will see and do things they have never done or seen before, for this generation will be great champions for my Kingdom"...

These words were fulfilled almost four years later, on June 6, 2015, when the American Pharoah won the Triple Crown Event. *ESPN News Online* reports:

With a final quarter-mile dash to the finish even faster than Secretariat's, American Pharoah ran into Triple Crown history with a dazzling display of speed and endurance in the Belmont Stakes.

Triple Crown winner Secretariat may have taken the 1973 Belmont by a record 31 lengths and in a record time of 2:24, but American Pharoah was faster to the finish over the final 440 yards. Big Red took 25 seconds; American Pharoah was .68 seconds quicker, going two furlongs in 24.32 seconds.[1]

There was more to the "Great Horse Prophecy," but I will address that in a later chapter of this book. Right now, I want to explain its importance and its connection to the D-Day comparison that God wants us to understand about the modern American Church.

It was a short time after I wrote the Trump prophecy that God gave me the "Great Horse Prophecy." Later on, I was listening to General Eisenhower's D-Day speech, and I heard the Lord say, "I want you to go back and rewrite this speech, addressing it to My Army." I did as I was told, and said what I felt the Holy Spirit wanted me to. I put these prophecies away for some time, until in 2015 there was a Triple Crown winner: American Pharoah. All at once, I realized that it had happened: The horse in the prophecy had arrived, and on June 6—the anniversary of D-Day! I immediately heard the Lord say that it was time to release the D-Day speech. Up to this point, I had never gone public with the prophecy of the horse. It had waited silently on my shelf for these years since it had been written. But now, the prophetic horse had arrived, and the Army was ready for the revised D-Day speech. We were now at two fulfillments out of three. I released the speech.

Only ten days later, Donald Trump announced that he was running for president. Within two weeks, all three of these things had come to pass. After four years of waiting to see how these words would materialize in the natural, I was finally able to witness prophecy fulfilled. I immediately began to ponder the scenario that was unfolding, and after some time of prayerful consideration, I wrote a letter to my fellow believers on June 20, 2015. For the sake of length, I will not include the full work here, but some of it is necessary to explain the significance of the "Great Horse Prophecy."

Hello brothers and sisters in the Lord. I wanted to share something with you I believe will be an encouragement to the Body of Christ, which the Lord led me to do back in 2011. I will keep this short. Prophet Paul Keith Davis always spoke of how the horse Secretariat represented the end-time Church. Well, while watching the movie (*Secretariat*), I kept hearing, "There's another one coming, there's another one coming." I then sat down to listen and write what the Lord was saying.

I wrote a prophetic word on 7-24-2011 called The Great Horse; it's a little lengthy, so I will just give you the main parts. What God was saying is that there is another Triple Crown winner coming and it would be a sign to the Church and this generation, that her time to break out is here. He would break records including Secretariat's, a sign to the Church it would do things never seen before.

American Pharoah broke Secretariat's time in the last turn, quarter mile: a sign that we are in the last turn coming into the home stretch toward the finish line. Does this mean we are in the end times? Yes. Does it mean we are at the end of time? NO! (More on this in the next chapter.) There is still much to be done, the end time harvest is just beginning where God will bring 1 billion souls into His kingdom before He returns. Well, it has happened, the Triple Crown, and I believe this was our sign for the American Church. (American Pharoah).

The word pharaoh means Great House; Royal Palace. He had the number 5, which is grace and redemption. The winning time was 2:26, which I believe is Revelation 2:26 ("To all who are victorious, who obey me to the very end, to them I will give authority over all the nations"). The jockey was from a 12-child family, and was the 12th Triple Crown win. 12 means God's government (will be established upon the earth).

You will see a lot of number 12 in the coming season. Donald Trump, 12th [Republican] candidate to enter the presidential race…

Some of the names in American Pharoah's bloodline—Empire Maker, Star of Goshen, Lord at War, Unbridled, Image of Reality, General, Key to the Kingdom—if these aren't prophetic signs then I don't know what is. There is an article posted on Elijahlist.com from Johnny Enlow and the revelation he got from the Triple Crown race, I encourage you to read it.

The article by Johnny Enlow that I referenced provided the following enlightening information:

Those with a Biblical foundation…remember the Pharaoh who would not allow the people of Israel to go free and thus came under severe judgment. However, it was also another Pharaoh hundreds of years before then, who…promoted Joseph to…ruler of Egypt. Without that Pharaoh, Joseph remains imprisoned and does not fulfill the promise…

The word Pharaoh actually means "big house" or "palace" and I think that is significant. I believe that American Pharoah winning speaks prophetically of a place and role that America is about to more fully step into as it relates to world affairs and the world economy.[2]

Enlow then goes on to explain that modern-day America is similar to Egypt in the days of Joseph. Besides the fact that we did not earn this status by some high moral code or by our deeds, our role in everything is due to the fact that God ordained us to be used for such a time as this. Enlow mentioned many other prophetic points in his article and, again, I recommend you read it.

Donald Trump announced on June 16, 2015, that he was running for president, and the Lord told me to go back and research June 16. I kept looking for a sign or trying to figure out what He meant, but I couldn't find anything. I was checking all throughout the news and every other source I could think of. Nothing. So I went back and prayed about it. I told Him, "Lord, I can't find it."

That was when He said, "Go back to World War II."

There it was again—the World War II component that He was beginning to use repeatedly. Once more, I went back to my research and found the connection. The Trump prophecy says that when he announces his running, it will be like the shot heard around the world.

June 16, 1945, was the day they made the decision to drop the atomic bomb. If that wasn't a shot heard around the world, I don't know what was.

D-Day

In the midst of all of this, God kept bringing my attention back to World War II. It seemed at every turn there was another comparison, another metaphor, another lesson He wanted His people to learn. Here is the modified D-Day speech that I felt the Lord prompting me to write two years before I was told to release it to the public.

Supreme Headquarters
Department of Spiritual Warfare
From: The Supreme Commander
To: The Army of God, Heaven's Invading Expeditionary Forces

Apostles, Prophets, Evangelists, Preachers and Teachers, Men and Women of the Army of God, you are about to embark upon a great crusade, toward which we have striven since all of creation. The eyes of the world and all of heaven are upon you. The hopes and prayers of liberty loving people everywhere march with you. In company with our brothers and sisters in arms on other fronts, you will bring about the destruction of the satanic war machine, the elimination of the demonic tyranny over the oppressed peoples of the earth, and security for ourselves in a free world.

Your task will not be an easy one. Your enemy is well trained, well equipped, and battle hardened. He will fight savagely.

BUT NOW IS THE TIME! Much has happened since the demonic triumphs of years past. The body of Christ have inflicted upon the demonic great defeats in the spiritual and natural realms. Our spiritual offensive has seriously reduced their strength in the air, and their capacity to wage war on the ground.

I have given you an overwhelming superiority in weapons for your warfare, and placed at your disposal great reserves of trained fighting men and women from the body of Christ.

THE TIDE HAS TURNED! The free men and women of my army are marching together to victory! I have full confidence in your courage, devotion to duty and skill in battle; we will accept nothing less than full victory! For this is a great and noble undertaking, AND THE VICTORY IS YOURS!
YOUR SUPREME COMMANDER, GOD

The D-Day Element for Modern-Day America and Its Church

In order to understand the parallels that God has given to me regarding D-Day and modern-day America, allow me to explain a bit about the actual battle on the beach that day and some of the preceding events.

The American government had gone to great lengths to throw enemy armies off track. They needed access to a place where they could invade France and gain ground in Europe. Entire decoy military bases made of false building structures, inflatable vehicles and tanks, and even sporting fake visits from General Patton himself to lend credibility, were constructed. In some places, tanks were made to look like mere trucks, while trucks and jeeps in other locations were built up to look like tanks. The same arts and crafts that might construct a modern-day set for an elaborate theatrical or Hollywood production were actually employed during this tumultuous, worldwide event to make German armies believe that the military was bulking up where it was not, and was neglecting areas it was actually fortifying.

Certain geographic locations were even blacked out when a German attack was anticipated, while a "fake" city was constructed nearby, causing German armies to bomb decoy cities during their attacks. False landing sites were even staged to throw off opposing forces' intelligence information. While all these tactics were being employed, German armies were beginning to fortify other areas. Much of their resources

69

had been moved, up to one hundred fifty miles away from Normandy and other beaches. Meanwhile, out of sight, far off shore, a ship with advanced weather forecasting equipment would eventually sit stationed on the water, informing Allied forces as to when the weather would offer an opportunity for attack upon the beaches for invasion.

While Allied forces busied themselves with their schemes of distraction and false fortification, German soldiers lived comfortably in the barracks along the beaches. Thanks to the great Allied efforts toward misinformation directed at the enemies' side, many did not believe they would be required to defend their location. They were fed regularly and lackadaisically kept watch. After all, the anticipated site of attacks was one hundred fifty miles away. Months went by with seemingly no activity at their location.

A visit from Erwin Rommel, however, to these locations immediately changed this for German soldiers. Omaha Beach's similarity in layout to Salerno Beach in Italy caused a certain sense of *déjà vu* to stir in Rommel's mind. Salerno Beach, not even a year earlier, had been overtaken by Allied forces under similar circumstances. He immediately began to reinforce the location, upgrading bunkers to defensive, concrete structures. Trenches filled with barbed wire and other defensive obstacles were installed across the beach, placed nearly every two yards, making the total about three thousand, seven hundred obstacles on this one beach. In certain places, land mines were even installed. Troops assigned to this location were increased to approximately twelve hundred.

In the meantime, while both armies were thus occupied, French resistance members were working behind the scenes to get information to the Allied forces. They had to be very cautious, as they were constantly under watch, which meant that messages to be passed on were often done so by way of subtleties such as codes hidden in paintings, messages via homing pigeons, or lyrics of songs. However, information about the reinforcements being made by Rommel was passed along through these channels as well as other forms of Allied intelligence. When members of this resistance were caught, they were executed or worse. But because of their successful attempts to sabotage trains, telegraph lines, and other German resources, communication was limited at Omaha which helped Allied efforts.

When the weather crew out on the ocean gave the news that June 6, 1944, might be the weather break Allied forces had been waiting for, the time to fight the battle at D-Day was upon them. Those who fought knew they were fighting for more than just their own country. The average age of a soldier on Omaha beach that day was twenty-two years. Some had signed up for military service, but many had been drafted. They were aware of the gravity of the situation, and many expected to die. By this time during WWII, the entire world was in such a state of upheaval that the soldiers knew the fate of the entire world was upon them.

Many lives were lost before the armed forces even hit the beach. "Swimming Tanks" (modified Sherman tanks) that had been built for launch in the water had only been tested in lakes, and the tossing of ocean waves caused them to fill with water and sink almost immediately, killing entire crews. Soldiers who had been fed a huge breakfast were rendered seasick in the water and were unable to recover and swim when weighted down by combat gear. Those who reached the shore faced defensive obstacles and a torrent of relentless ammunition spray.

The enemy was armed with MG42s—the world's fastest machine gun at the time. About twelve hundred of these guns appeared out of openings in the recently reinforced concrete structure facing the beach. Firing up to fifteen hundred bullets per minute (twenty-five per second at over two thousand miles per hour), these were devastatingly faster than the guns that Allied forces were armed with at the time. This demoralizing sound of rapid fire became known as "Hitler's Zipper." These soldiers were faced with the task of either taking these guns out as soon as possible or facing continued, quickly mounting casualties.

Allied hopes hinged on the air attack that would soon give them the advantage. When thirteen thousand bombs were to be dropped from overhead, this would give them their opportunity to rush the barracks and overtake the base. However, visibility from the sky was not optimal, and pilots who hesitated dropped their explosives up to a mile away from their mark, causing the blasts to miss their targets completely. Members of the forces who were attempting to join the battle by parachute became tangled in the 'chutes' lines upon landing in the water and drowned.

Simultaneously, Elite forces attempting to take out artillery bases found that they had been deceived by what turned out to be the enemies' own decoy base, while the real artillery had been waiting at the beach. Sea water was running red with blood and defeat was looming. Allied troops were having trouble breaking through the obstacles on the beach. Casualties were so high that strategies were lost and guidance was missing. Individuals began to feel like the last ones standing in a fragmented, mission-less battle. Many felt alone.

When Norman "Dutch" Cota, age fifty-one at the time, arrived in the second wave of the attempted invasion, he immediately assessed the situation as dire and in need of leadership. One of the highest-ranking officers on the beach that day, he wasted no time in rallying men to a cause and directing them. It is said that he motivated them by saying, "Gentlemen, we are being killed on the beaches. Let us go inland and be killed."[3] His honesty about the situation allowed men to get a realistic grip on fear and keep the mission in perspective. With fresh direction and another gust of momentum, the battle finally began to change hands.

Cota led the soldiers to the seawall, where they used Bangalore torpedoes to cut through obstacles and take ground. The casualties did not stop there, but the new leader challenged the men to keep going. With this newfound momentum, nearby forces that had been undecided about *where* to fight joined in this battle and tipped the scale. Allied forces finally won the costly victory.

Understanding the D-Day Comparison

When I make comparisons to D-Day, I am by no means downplaying the sacrifices made on that day. I realize that it was indeed a bloody battle, and I'm not likening our current American situation to the events of June 6, 1944, in the physical realm. Rather, I'm talking about a spiritual battle that is raging throughout our planet right now. And, as it did on D-Day, the future of the world depends on what we do in that battle today.

As stated, the average age of a soldier on that day was twenty-two years. Our youngest generations are always the most vulnerable to attack. They are the most easily influenced and the most easily misled. They are also, however, often the most passionate and hence the most influential. They are the dreamers, the activists, the makers of statements, the most vocal. They are the future and they *know it.* Just like the soldiers on the beach that day, some volunteer for the tasks they're heading toward, but others are called, or drafted.

The hesitation of the pilots dropping thirteen thousand bombs on the beach that day caused them to miss their mark by almost a mile. It is important to remember that when it is time to take action, that time is always *now.* Moments are of the essence when God calls us to action. Even seconds wasted while we are deciding whether or not to be obedient can make a huge difference in the battle to which we are called.

The German soldiers who had lived on the beach in the bunkers, comfortable, secure in the idea that they would not be required to defend their location, are somewhat like those who are corrupt: those evil dwellers who have grown so comfortable in places of power and do not expect to have to give up their seats. They have lived like there is no tomorrow, no day of reckoning, no "game changer" on the horizon.

They have lived like the man in the Isaiah 56:11–12:

Yea, they are greedy dogs which can never have enough,
and they are shepherds that cannot understand: they all look to
their own way, every one for his gain, from his quarter.
Come ye, say they, I will fetch wine, and we will fill ourselves
with strong drink; and to morrow shall be as this day,
and much more abundant.

The shift in power and convictions within the American population over the last few years has caused them alarm—stirred their comfort zone, so to speak—and they have begun to fortify their locations. Understand that just like the German soldiers at Omaha that day, they have access to insurmountably powerful weapons. They have already put up a forceful struggle, and will continue to do so. A habitation is not taken away from forces of darkness without a fight. Ground that is gained must be held. What if the soldiers who made it to the seawall had then turned back? All the lives lost would have been lost in vain. And whether or not they realized it in the heat of battle, when they hit that marker, the battle was almost won.

Soldiers on the ground that day were surrounded by fallen companions—some were deceased, others were calling for medics or other help, still others were even shouting for their mothers. What a demoralizing state that must have been for those who were still trying to achieve victory! Sometimes, looking around and seeing only fallen soldiers can create an overwhelming sense of panic concerning what we are trying to accomplish. Looking around, trying to find a voice to follow, and seeing no one willing to lead can make the situation seem even more hopeless.

"Dutch" Cota was a regular guy. While he was one of the highest-ranking officers there, he was also one of the later to arrive and one of the oldest as well. Some might not have been able to pull him out of a crowd as the one who would be able to tip the scale in favor of the Allied forces that day. But he was said to be fearless, and he challenged the men not to give up. He was more than someone who was merely in the right place at the right time. He was able to assess what the troops lacked (leadership) and then stepped in to fill that gap. His brutal honesty to the men about their situation motivated them to take action even when things seemed hopeless. His intervention was vital in saving many lives and attaining a victory that at that point appeared impossible.

The French Resistance, who had been feeding info to the Allied forces behind the scenes, were regular, everyday people who wanted to see good prevail over evil. They were unsung heroes who made a difference.

And, like He used these people, God can use you. If you are willing to honestly assess a situation and place yourself in the gap, God can take a bad situation and turn it around for the good of many. Remember that in spite of all the weapons on the beach that day—as well as all the preparation that had been made for the battle, all the ingenuity, expense, planning, and even the sabotage efforts of the French resistance—what really carried the plan through were the men on the ground. Without the actual people willing to place themselves in the situation and carry out orders, no matter the cost, no victory would have been attained in that crucial hour, and the entire WWII would have possibly had a different outcome. Success was achieved by those who stepped up and answered their call.

And when the battle began to turn around, nearby forces who were not sure which battle to join came in as reinforcements. As you stand for what is right, others will follow. You may feel alone, surrounded by the fallen, and without direction. But as you answer your call and step into the role that God has given you, you will find that others may soon follow suit. Nearby forces that hadn't decided to join your battle now may stand for your cause as well.

It is the remnant that is going to take—*and hold*—ground. The Lord has showed me that just as England was the hub from which D-Day was launched, America will be the location where this modern-day spiritual battle will be stationed for the end-time harvest. America is going to be central when this victory is achieved for the spiritually oppressed people across the earth. So, this is where the Church must be ready to be effective right now.

The Army of God and the Body of Christ

The Army of God and the Body of Christ, to me, are not entirely the same. The Body of Christ, the way I see it, is like individuals in boot camp, where they are trained and nurtured until mature enough for battle. When promoted, they then also become part of the Army of God. The Army of God is a force to be reckoned with, made up of the mature, progressive members of the Body of Christ who are ready for battle and empowered with God's authority.

On D-Day, some of the men had been out in their boats for three days, and were seasick before they ever hit the beaches. The Body of Christ is metaphorically on those ships right now. God has showed me that most of the Church is too focused on the storm. They are being tossed about, back and forth, and they are seasick—unable to advance to the next step.

I get a lot of emails and communications from people who are scared to death. They know something is coming, and they don't know how to prepare. They are like those stuck on the boats, getting tossed about because they are too absorbed with the waves that are stirring. Anybody who has ever worked with me in the fire service knows that I'm very mission oriented. We must always focus on the mission and keep advancing. We can't let obstacles or storms get in the way.

Others have been promoted out of these ships, and they are on the landing craft. No longer seasick, they are heading toward their goal—but all they see are the obstacles placed to keep the armory from coming onto the beach. They are frozen with fear and unaware of their own capabilities. Because of this, they are unable to move forward.

Then we have the Army of God. These members of the body of

Christ have actually landed and are not focused on the storm. They're on the beach, taking ground, and holding that ground. They see where needs are and step into those gaps. They are rallying to the cause and pressing in, no matter what.

That's the difference.

America is going to be prosperous; America is going to flourish because of the seeds that it has sewn; and America will be central as the Gospel is spread from this point forward. God has told me this. This will be the end-time harvest. And it will have a domino effect. Just like the events on Omaha Beach that day in 1944, whatever happens in America will ripple throughout the earth.

If you are taking ground, *press in.* If you are stuck at an obstacle, look around you and get help. *Don't retreat.* Take ground and hold it at all costs, and understand that no matter how unqualified you may feel, God can and will use you.

NOW IS THE TIME! Advance! Do not retreat. I like what General George Patton said: "I don't like paying for the same real-estate twice."

Engaging in Ungodly Warfare

God speaks to everybody differently, and He talks to me in fire station lingo. The Lord has told me, "Mark, my Church is bleeding out; as are my people. I want you to go in and do spiritual triage. Give them the message, and if they don't listen, *do not* get involved in ungodly warfare, such as arguing. Those who you see making conflict within My Army are to be considered in the black. They are spiritually dead. I will deal with them on My own. Keep moving. Because there are too many people out there who are in the red, yellow, and the green, the walking wounded, some of whom have even been injured by the Church. These will listen to the message, but more importantly, they will *act* on it."

If you really apply this to your daily relationship with God and your effectiveness as a Christian, then taking action, with a "boots-on-the-ground" approach, makes spreading the Gospel seem much more feasible. You would no longer be worried about who you're offending, how foolish you may appear to others, or how you're going to defend yourself. It simplifies the whole commission. And isn't that what it's really about?

> *And let us not be weary in well doing:*
> *for in due season we shall reap, if we faint not.*
> GALATIANS 6:9

Don't be discouraged in this: Not everybody you try to reach will listen. You may not be the specific person they'll be willing to listen to. The person coming behind you might reap the harvest of seeds you planted. You don't always know who God's going to work through and in what ways. Just keep your eyes on the task before you and let Him take care of the rest.

Intellect vs. Intellect

Much of the battle that we fight right now is actually that of intellect against intellect. Some of it is a mere byproduct of people still learning to discern which way to go, but some of it is more overt and deliberate. The Lord has given me this equation: A religious spirit + a legalistic spirit = a critical spirit.

This equation is actually at the root of a trend of distraction used by the enemy to divide the Church against itself.

At the heart of this movement, people literally attack each other with the Bible, using their intellect, fueled by what they *feel* is the interpretation of Scripture. Many of them think they are doing God's work, but they're really operating in the flesh. They think that their scholarly knowledge of the scriptural *words* means that they, in their finite understanding, can quote the *heart of God*. But, the Lord is saying, "No, you're

PART TWO: THE MESSAGE

off base. You are making My Church a house divided. You people who create a rift in my house don't even know Me."

God is asking us to set aside our agendas and seek His will for our lives, our households, and our country. He is ready to see us refocus our energy on the battle, and not on petty arguments and gratuitous friction. God has specifically instructed me not to engage in warfare that He did not ordain. He wants to see His army unite and gain ground again.

Late in August, God told me to write the following "Declaration of Unity." He wanted it written because He was tired of the Church fighting against itself. His will is to see us channel our energy into constructive behavior that has eternal value. It was intended to be filled in individually and signed as a contract agreed upon by believers as a commitment to God, their pledge to Him.

Declaration of Unity

I, _____, in the name of Jesus, decree and declare, according to Matthew 18:19, that I will be in unity with my brothers and sisters in the Army of God and all the forces of Heaven. That I will support and defend the Word of God and His army, with all of Heaven, against all enemies from the Kingdom of Darkness, even unto supreme sacrifice.

I will not fire upon those in the Army of God, but will direct my fire upon the enemy, and the enemy alone. I will protect my brothers and sisters in God's army, from any assault that the enemy may launch. I will bear true faith and allegiance to the same, on and off the battlefield.

I will obey the orders of the Supreme Commander of the Army of God, and the orders of the officers appointed over me, according to Ephesians 4:11, the Government of God, and the uniform regulations founded on God's throne of righteousness and justice. I decree it and declare it on earth as it is in Heaven. So be it, Amen!

Are You in God's Army?

Can you agree to these terms today? Will you not only be part of the modern-day Church, but stand up to be a part of God's Army? Will you graduate from the waters to the landing craft and proceed toward shore? Will you heed the words that the Lord has given and begin to prepare for the battle of D-Day that lies ahead in the spiritual realm?

It is time for the remnant to gather and ready ourselves for the task before us, without focusing on obstacles or irrelevant disputes that will divide an army against itself.

Onward Christian Soldiers!

The following is a prophecy I wrote on January 28, 2016, entitled "Defeated Enemy":

The Spirit of God says, "There is an army arising from the dust and ashes from many battles and enemy clashes. This army that's arising is coming in my glory and light, and the battle that's about to unfold shall put the enemy to flight. For my army is about to hit the beaches and shores of every country and nation afar, and they shall drive back the army of darkness at the sound of my shofar! For my army will be young and old; and will save over 1 billion souls!"

The Spirit of God says, "There is nothing that the enemy can do to stop this that I, the Lord God, have started, for it is now the time for the army of darkness to be departed. For the souls of this nation and all over the world are crying out to me. My Army! Bring them in, and I will save, deliver, and comfort thee. Arise; Army of God! Arise! Your work is not complete, for the kingdom of darkness is in for its biggest surprise, complete and utter defeat! Arise; my Army! Get in the fight, I say with great emphasis! Overtake, terminate, and destroy the army of darkness with Extreme Prejudice!"

—Your Supreme Commander, God

The Shofar

The Lord told me that He would save one billion souls.

One billion souls!

He gave me this word in January of 2016. What I did not know at the time, however, was that He would appoint certain key players to lead an organized blowing of the shofar on the day of election later the same year. God is truly faithful. He brings everything full circle. The shofar turned out to be a very significant sign historically and spiritually representing the trump of God. Its meanings are many, and could easily be their own topic for another book, but allow me to elaborate on a few here:

- Made of a ram's horn, it is associated with the ram used as the sacrifice the day Abraham took his only son to be sacrificed as an act of obedience to God. The shofar then reminds us of God's provision in our obedience, and that God has given *His only Son* to us as the ultimate sacrifice.

- It was blown as armies headed into spiritual battle, during worship, or at other spiritually significant times—for example, its blast will be heard at the final judgment. It was also sounded to herald messages, to coronate kings, or to alert Israelites to battle. This particular purpose significant to America's current position, because the shofar basically served as a call to arms, or a sign that a change of leadership was taking place.

- It was used at the battle of Jericho, when the sound of its blast brought down the walls (much like when the Lord granted the red side victory over the "blue wall" on Election Day 2016).

- It was sounded as the Lord appeared in a thick cloud before Moses (see Exodus 19:16).
- At the end times, its call of the shofar will gather His elect from the four winds (Matthew 24:31).

God is calling you to be in His army. He is bringing change across this country and is looking for those who will march to His beat and follow His orders. Are you ready to take a stand? Are you ready to commit to His will and watch lives be transformed?

chapter five

The Sands of Time

Human Actions Impact God's Reactions

Does God change? No. Malachi 3:6 clearly backs up this fact: "For I am the Lord, I change not; therefore ye sons of Jacob are not consumed."

God is the same yesterday, today, and forever. He is I AM. He does not change.

He does, however, change His course of action at times in response to man's actions. In the story of Jonah, He told Jonah to go and preach to the city of Nineveh with the warning that it would be destroyed in forty days if those who lived there did not turn from wickedness.

So Jonah arose, and went unto Nineveh, according to the word of the Lord. Now Nineveh was an exceeding great city of three days' journey. And Jonah began to enter into the city a day's journey, and he cried, and said, Yet forty days, Nineveh shall be overthrown. So the people of Nineveh believed God, and proclaimed a fast, and put on sackcloth, from the greatest of them even to the least of them. For word came unto the king of Nineveh, and he arose from his throne, and he laid his robe from him, and covered him with a sackcloth, and sat in ashes. And he caused it to be proclaimed and published through Nineveh by the decree of the king and his nobles, saying, Let neither man nor beast, herd nor flock, taste any thing: let them not feed, nor drink water: But let man and beast be covered in sackcloth, and cry mightily unto God: yea, let them turn every one from his evil way, and from the violence that is in their hands. Who can tell if God will turn and repent, and turn away from his fierce anger, that we perish not? And God saw their works, that they turned from their evil way; and God repented of the evil, that he had said that he would do unto them; and he did it not.

JONAH 3:3–10

Notice in this story that a message is delivered from God. God tells people what is coming: disaster. Their time is up. The people's response is dramatic. They don't make a casual commitment to do something differently later on at their own convenience. They change *drastically*. Even their *king* makes radical changes. Transformation takes place within their government from the top all the way down to the least of the population. The king, himself, calls for repentance from and mourning for their evil from not only all people, but even their animals. A fast is called across the city. When God sees the *sincere reformation* that Jonah's warning has brought, He actually "repents of the evil" He was about to send their way and saves them.

Important to understand is that while God does not change, He sometimes alters the course of events, even allowing His children to suffer harder or longer for their own good if He sees fit. This is no secret hidden in shadows. He, Himself, asserts this in Jeremiah 18:7–10:

At what instant I shall speak concerning a nation, and concerning a kingdom, to pluck up, and to pull down, and to destroy it; If that nation, against whom I have pronounced, turn from their evil, I will repent of the evil that I thought to do unto them. And at what instant I shall speak concerning a nation, and concerning a kingdom, to build and to plant it; If it do evil in my sight, that it obey not my voice, then I will repent of the good, wherewith I said I would benefit them.

Why All This Didn't Happen in 2012

The second half of the "Great Horse Prophecy" that I talked about during my discussion of the Secretariat racehorse is below. Written July 24, 2011:

> The Spirit of God says, "The Church didn't recognize the last sign I gave them in Secretariat, but this time they shall, for the eyes of the world shall be upon this horse and My Church. People might say, "Why is God interested in a horse?" Because he is My creation, and he is a sign that I am giving My people for this generation. The old saying goes, records were made to be broken, and this horse and My Church shall set records that will never be broken. Watch for the horse, watch for the horse. 2012 will be the year of the horse.

Secretariat itself was a prophetic sign of the end-time Church that would come from behind and surpass, with an enlarged heart for God and strength to win the race. What I wrote above, as I have said, was written in 2011. At that time, I had thought all of this would happen in 2012. I didn't go public with the "Great Horse Prophecy" because, although I was certain God was giving me this message *for this time*, something still felt off about the actual year 2012.

However, the revelation of the "Commander-in-Chief" Trump prophecy followed so closely by the "Great Horse Prophecy" gave me a sense of momentum, causing me to know in the core of my being that God was doing something. Therefore, when He prompted me with the year 2012, I wrote it, but I put it on a shelf to wait and see what God would do.

And when I rewrote the D-Day speech, I placed it on the shelf with the "Great Horse Prophecy."

When Trump didn't announce that he was going to run for presidency, and there wasn't a Triple Crown winner, I thought I had missed the mark. I wasn't sure how it had been possible, since I *knew* God had given me that word, but I trusted Him. I knew that there was a reason He would give me these words, even if I had somehow missed the timing. I thought maybe He was using this to teach me something for another time. Some sort of practice or training, maybe.

In 2015, I kept watching the Triple Crown races. I thought maybe I would learn something that would help me piece together the essence of the "Great Horse." I still knew that the Word I had been given was from God; I just thought I missed the timing on it. On June 6 of that year, I was on the phone with my sister when, out of the blue, she asked what day it was.

All of a sudden it hit me. "Man, it's D-Day."

And as you know, that is the day I released the speech, and ten days later, Donald Trump announced that he was running for president. I had written all three of these works—D-Day, Trump, and the Great Horse—all within a very short time of each other, nearly four years earlier. I had been sure God was moving quickly, because at the time He had given me the works in such rapid succession. I thought this haste was because these events were to happen soon, so I had said "2012." When it didn't happen, I thought God must be teaching me obedience. Perhaps *that* was the lesson.

But now, after four years, all of these prophecies were tying together before my very eyes, one right after another!

I was astounded. I kept saying, "Lord, I thought I missed these. I thought I missed these prophecies."

And I finally had my answer. I heard Him say, "All of this was supposed to happen in 2012, but My people were not ready. They needed four more years of the current administration in order to get a righteous anger, rise up, and say 'enough is enough.' For this reason, I held it off."

The "Commander-in-Chief Prophecy" about Trump couldn't actually begin to play out until Donald Trump *announced that he was running for president*. When he made this announcement in 2015, he unleashed part of the prophecy. When American Pharoah won the Triple Crown, he was a symbol to the Church.

Further into my revelation about God's timing, I was praying one afternoon, and I felt the Spirit of the Lord directing me to take a closer look at the winner of the 2012 Triple Crown. This would have been the horse I thought I was writing about in the "Great Horse Prophecy." The horse that had been slated to win was named "I'll Have Another." He had won the first two races. One more win and he would hold the Triple Crown. He was the strongest contender for the third race until a tendon injury caused him not to run. Since winning the Triple Crown requires victory at all three races, there was no Triple Crown winner that year.

When I saw that the horse's name was "I'll Have Another," at first I laughed it off as someone's cute idea of tongue-in-cheek humor, as in "I'll have another drink" (or something quippish like that).

But the Lord answered, "No. That's not what it means. It means, I'll have *another one coming*. This is not the one. There is another that will follow at the right time."

This confirmed to me that, even though these events did not happen in 2012, God had a plan that He was carrying out in His own perfect timing. Trump did not announce that he would run in 2012. The Great Horse did not arrive in 2012. Instead, our answer was, "I'll have another." This explained to me why I felt so strongly about the year 2012, and yet so unsettled about the timing as well. Four years after the journey began, *at last*, I was starting to understand. An acquaintance once told me that when God gives us a prophetic word, He seldom fulfills it right away. It is often *years* before we see the fruits of the divinatory. She was right.

God waited. He did it on purpose. He did it, because He was waiting for our complete attention. He wanted a generation of people to be ready, waiting to see Him move. He wanted us in prayer as a nation. He wanted us united, revolutionary, and ready for *change*. And this is not the first time that He has acted in such a way.

He is merciful, and He doesn't want the train to leave without anyone. He wants His people to be ready, and He often waits for us to respond before setting things into motion. Remember that when God was planning to destroy the evil cities of Sodom and Gomorrah, as recorded in the book of Genesis, Abraham asked God if He would spare the cities for the sake of any inside who were not evil. He began his bargaining with the Almighty at fifty righteous individuals, and worked his way down to ten. God agreed that, if even as few as ten upright people could be found within the cities' limits, they it would be spared.

> *And he said, Oh let not the Lord be angry,*
> *and I will speak yet but this once:*
> *Peradventure ten shall be found there.*
> *And he said, I will not destroy it for ten's sake.*
> Genesis 18:32

> *The Lord is not slack concerning his promise, as some men count*
> *slackness; but is longsuffering to us-ward, not willing that any*
> *should perish, but that all should come to repentance.*
> 2 Peter 3:9

God will also wait on things if He is dealing with rebellious and contemptible people who refuse to give Him authority. In Numbers, we see where God delayed His plans of blessing due to rebellion within His people. He would not allow the people to inherit the Promised Land until their hearts were ready.

Surely they shall not see the land which I sware unto their fathers,
neither shall any of them that provoked me see it.
NUMBERS 14:23

The Israelites could have gained access to this land so much sooner if they had believed God's promises and followed His direction. But they were rebellious and murmured at every turn, and in the end, they even accused God of bringing them to the wilderness so that they would die by the sword!

God was tired of His people's rebellion, contempt, lack of gratitude, and disbelief—even after He had repeatedly shown them signs of His strength, power, and provision.

Sound like any nation you know today?

God's response was to delay His plan of sending His people into the Promised Land. He actually postponed the day that their lives would change for the better, when victory would finally be theirs—*the moment when their destiny would finally be upon them.*

Your carcases shall fall in this wilderness; and all that were
numbered of you, according to your whole number, from twenty
years old and upward, which have murmured against me.
NUMBERS 14:29

The Lord waited for a fresh, new generation of believers to arise. (By the way, there's that age again: twenty years.) He allowed age, time, and even death as a cleansing agent to purge the people of those who were unable to believe, unwilling to dream, incapable of seeing a new world on the horizon because they were just too "stuck in their own heads," as it were, to hear His voice. In short, He was tired of trying to teach stubborn old dogs new tricks. But, when the people were finally ready and a fresh, youthful, visionary generation had emerged, He led them into the Promised Land *just as He had said He would* so long before it actually came to be.

So, Does that Mean We're at the End of Time? NO!

In the final line of the Trump prophecy, God told me that even mainstream news media would be captivated by this man and begin to agree with him. Countless numbers of people have asked what it would take to make this drastic change occur. Many who point fingers at what they call a corrupt media system jump to the conclusion that a terrible disaster will occur, bringing the entire country, including news media, to their knees. This is possible, and the enemy certainly has the weapons for such an event. But does it really need to come to that? Will it?

If my people…

I feel the wings of revival—and by this, I really mean a sudden Great Awakening like those our globe has witnessed in the past through the ministries of youthful, passionate leaders who take the Gospel outside the box the Church has historically placed it in. I'm talking about a movement unchained to the traditional church buildings emergent with people who have never even been serious about God. I'm referring to that new, fresh generation purged of all the old, faithless, unbelieving, and tired pew-warmers who call themselves the Body of Christ but haven't seen Him in years. I mean a generation like the one God allowed to inherit the Promised Land.

And when it happens, it is not going to take place in the drowsy, exhausted church that has "grandfathered in" a whole bunch of suits.

I believe God will clean house all over the place: within the government, within the church, and definitely within the news media. Sadly, some churches will close for lack of finances, but home churches will start springing up all over the place. Politicians will be asked to step down, and some will possibly be arrested. I think we will even see some large organizations go under. The systems of power in this country are about to fall under judgment. So, what of this disaster some foretell will be the pinnacle that brings the news media into humble agreement with God's Anointed? I don't necessarily believe it will happen. I'm not saying we won't have issues, but as far as an economic collapse or other calamity that some people have been prophesying… No. I don't believe we're facing that. Will there be turbulence as we move ahead? Yes, there *could be*. But an all-out catastrophe does not *have to be* the guaranteed method God will use.

God gave me a word in July of 2016 called "Operation Let My People Go" regarding the counterfeit timeline that people are prophesying to keep believers from being effective. An excerpt of this word follows:

The Spirit of God says, "The timeline, the counterfeit timeline that they have used, you shall see it and how it's been abused. For the counterfeit timeline that they have used to lead my people astray, will be exposed and seen because my remnant people have prayed. You people who speak with time and truth that bend, thinking you have encircled my body and sealed them in, hoping it's now their end. For you are saying they are no longer a threat for they accepted a truth that bends. Woe to you for you forgot about my remnant and that's my surprise, and now it's your end and it shall be your demise! For the counterfeit spiritual compass that is pulling and magnetizing my people off course as it be, will be turned back by my true army, and pointed true north, and back to me."

If My People

Many people are promoting a timeline of doom and gloom right now. They are listening to the enemy and prophesying as if catastrophe were God's plan—*and it's not*. God's plan is not to punish or decimate America. Remember the story I referred to above, in which God told Abraham that He would spare the city if even as few as ten righteous people could be found? Well, you *do* know that we have more than ten righteous people in America, don't you?

Many of us are stuck in a mindset that has us wanting to see America burn because of the sin we observe around us: the blasphemy, the laws that don't align with our religious convictions, and so on. Why are we trying to call God's wrath down based upon our personal agendas?

I hear it every day.

America is not under judgment. The Bible says "if my people"—and when it says "*my* people," it is referring to the Church, not "*the* people" of any specific nation generically. It is *His* people who have some serious repenting to do! Many of us are in such a hurry to see the wrath of God fall on "those other people who are sinning," we are losing sight of the fact that *we* are the very people upon whom we are attempting to call down His wrath!

Contrary to popular belief, judgment is not coming to the people in the general American public. It is heading for our government systems and the Church. It is *we* who must repent. The Church will be found guilty for these sins that we say are coming under judgment. Only one example is all of the babies who die by abortion each year. The blood of those babies is not on "America's hands," but on "the Church's hands." How so? We are called to be the spiritual and moral compass of our country, are we not? We, the Army of God, are responsible to lead the way. So, if you want to know why America is in the shape it's in, look at the Church, and you will find your answer. (More on this later, in the discussion of "the Church without spot or wrinkle.")

What will be the eye-opening event that brings the media into play with the last line of the Trump prophecy? What will it take for the United States news media to come to this? I believe it's going to be when all the "good" comes flooding in again. When the events that the "America, America" prophecy talks of are all coming to pass, it will be undeniable. After all, when the economy is booming, the economy thrives, the military is where it needs to be, our borders are secure, and revival flows through the land: How can there be any refuting those facts? How could the media possibly continue to lie? They will be forced to acknowledge Trump's insight at that point. Once people start to realize that these things are happening, whether or not the media wants to be truthful about it, the media will have to choose between agreeing with Trump or reporting with such transparent fallacy that they will be written off or scoffed at by the general public. It will be a day of reckoning for them when the public demands new accountability from those who stand behind the news station pulpits.

But we, as believers, need to keep our eyes upward and know that God is in control. He is already beginning to turn things around for us.

So many believers during times of trial or transition begin stepping into public view, panicking and connecting circumstances around them to the book of Revelation. This spurs on a sort of fear factor, causing people to shut down and live in a state of anxiety. Just because a word is prophetic does not mean that it has to instill dread in the people it was written to.

It happens all the time that I get people approaching me, citing such doomsday prophecies as "the New World Order is about to take over," a "natural disaster will wipe America out," or other such catastrophic predictions. It seems that many people occupy their time and focus consistently on the book of Revelation, as if in some strange attempt to animate the end-times prophecies by pointing out our current circumstances' potential for disaster, instead of letting the Lord reveal His plan in His own timing.

Time out guys… I understand some things appear as though they are lining up with Revelation, but heaven does not exist in the same realm of time as we do.

And don't think for one second that the forces of evil don't have the resources in place to make some seriously disastrous things happen, because they do. The enemy may be trying to bring in some devastatingly sinister agendas—make no mistake—but if we truly believe that He who is in us is greater than he who is in the world, as 1 John 4:4 states, then we have to *stop focusing on the storm*!

We have to get our minds off the obstacles so we can really be used by God and not distracted the moment we're called to action!

The Fourth Reich, ISIS

Another prophecy, which I wrote on October 19, 2016, entitled "Full Circle" reads:

The Spirit of God says, "Russia, that's right, Russia. I will use Russia, the United States of America and her allies, to take on the 4th Reich called ISIS. For it has come full circle again, that's right, again. The New World Order is trying to rise and take its place, just like they did in WWII, using the Nazis. They will try again using ISIS. For this plague is spreading but not for long, for they will be wiped out for their wrongs. For just as in WWII, America and her allies came in from the west and Russia from the east, so shall it be again to slay this so-called beast, and it will be brought down to the least. Some will say, 'Why would I use Russia?' Am I not the God of the cosmos? I will use anyone and any nation I choose, whether some like it or not! I will not be put in a box!"

The Spirit of God says, "The ties that were severed between America and Russia, will begin to mend and they will take on this so-called Goliath and with one stone shall slay it and all those that are behind it. For it is not just ISIS they will fight, but the Elite, the Globalists, and the Illuminati who will be exposed by My light. For they are an enemy to the world and My agenda. They shall fall with a mighty blow, so that My Gospel will begin to flow. For they wear their flag as if it were a prayer shawl, so they will be taken down with my Shock and Awe! For freedom and liberty will begin to ring, and the people will begin to sing, as healing and light come from my wings. My people rejoice and shout, for My Gospel is coming and will go through all the earth, and all the nations will know this is why My America was birthed!"

Is there going to be World War III? Maybe someday. It can't be ruled out, but I don't think it's coming anytime soon. Are we going to have some military engagements? Absolutely. I believe there definitely will be with ISIS. ISIS is only the latest face on an age-old enemy, which currently surfaces as the fourth *Reich* (again, bringing us back to comparison with WWII).

The Lord has told me that we will work with Russia again just as we did in World War II. Russia will come in from the east, with us approaching from the West, and we will defeat ISIS just as we did the Nazis. We've done it before, and have come full circle since World War II. We have seen this movie already. The New World Order has been trying to raise its ugly head through the use of ISIS as the fourth *Reich*. But God has said, "No, this is not happening, the enemy has their timeline, and I have Mine." It may seem like things are escalating out of control, but God will not be bullied into the enemy's timeline...and things are *never* out of His control.

In the timeline that we are in now, ISIS will be defeated, and America will be prosperous. We're not seeing the New World Order take over; we are seeing it being taken down. America is going to flourish because of the seeds it has sewn from its beginning. This blessed country is central for the reaping of the end-time harvest, and our spiritual revival will ripple outward throughout the entire earth. The Luciferian reign is coming to an end! I am a firm believer that we are about to see the New World Order come crashing down.

This is the point where some people disagree with me, but it is because they have a hard time letting go of that counterfeit timeline they're attached to.

Understand that every generation has its moment of impending doom. Remember Y2K? That's just one recent example of the time markers to which people nail certain deadlines of disaster. A simple study reveals that at least once per decade, the history of our country has been riddled with events that made those enduring them absolutely certain that the end of the earth was approaching.

Don't think for a moment that the World War II generation didn't deal with the same New World Order we currently see attempting to gain control, because it was trying to upsurge even back then. Just remember, it *can* be taken on, it *can* be beaten, and it *will* be.

"Shatter and Scatter," a prophetic word the Lord gave me on June 12, 2016, reads in full:

> The Spirit of God says, "The Illuminati and ISIS have emerged and are attacking the pulse of this nation, for they are responsible for the list of assassinations. For the New World Order is shaking and quaking, for they will go down in flames a-blazing. For they are trying to kill this nation before my chosen one takes office through depopulation, finances, and assassinations, stop the attacks to the pulse of this nation."
>
> The Spirit of God says, "The Illuminati, I the Lord God shall expose the Illuminati because of who they want to be. They shall say we will be the world leaders like a shot! Not so fast, for I, the Lord God will shatter you like a clay pot. Shattered and

Scattered, my wind will send you back to the one who sent you. For you think you are wise craving power, money, and the prize. You so-called wise have been fooled by the lust and the lure of the prize to the point that the one who sent you now seeks his payment, and this, too, you will soon realize. For your days are numbered and short, Woe to you when you have to stand before him and report. For this will be for all to see for when you serve the god of this world it will bring you low, repent or you shall be cast into the fire below."

The Spirit of God says, "Why do the prophets of doom and gloom keep saying that this is the end? For they are misreading the season of time we are in. For those that keep speaking this with words that bend, are aiding the enemy making the people lay down their arms, give up, lose hope, stop fighting and saying, 'We will just ride this out to the end.' For you are never to stop fighting or lay down your arms for any reason. Stop listening to those who commit spiritual treason. For life and death are in the power of the tongue, for this treasonous talk is even affecting the young. Stop aiding the enemy and start talking about what I the Lord God and my Army are going to do. Grab the enemy by the throat and make him fluster. Look him in the eyes and say, 'Is that all you can muster?' Choose this day whom you will serve, for I have given you the victory and the choice is yours."

Your Supreme Commander, God

The Sands of Time

You may remember the phrase, "Like sands through the hourglass, so are the days of our lives..."[4]

It's true that, to us, time is here for literally moments and then it is forever gone, just as that phrase depicts. It's important to remember, however, that the hand of God has the power to reach out and flip the hourglass over, or turn it on its side and stop time completely. He did just that for Joshua. He is not limited by our definition of time, nor is He intimidated by where we see the future headed in our own finite minds. The Bible says a thousand years is like a day to God.

> *But, beloved, be not ignorant of this one thing,*
> *that one day is with the Lord as a thousand years,*
> *and a thousand years as one day.*
> 2 PETER 3:8

Humor me for just a moment while we play a little numbers game. The Lord told me one day while I was praying about all of this, "Mark, do you realize it took Me six days to build the earth?" That could be compared to six thousand years to God. We would then be in the year 5777: only five and three quarters' day into that week. If that were the case, then there would still be 223 years left. Now, please understand that I'm *not* saying that's how long it will be before He comes back. He could come back right now, even as I write this, or He could wait five hundred more years. My point is that *no man knows the hour*, and those looking to calculate a number within the realm of their own understanding will manage to find a way—but sometimes people become so obsessed with worrying about whether we are in the end times that they begin wasting the only time we do know that we have, which is the *present*. That then becomes its own obstacle.

When people spend their time prophesying gloom and doom, they are boasting the plans of the enemy and magnifying the evil intent toward God's own. The Lord has even told me they are committing spiritual treason when they do this, because they're actually *aiding* the enemy. (Yes, you read that correctly.)

People who spend exorbitant amounts of time and energy giving prophecies of despair and mass destruction are empowering the enemy as they incite alarm and demoralize the Body, essentially rendering them cowards in the heat of battle. And that couldn't possibly be God's plan. I cannot tell you how many times I've heard someone say, "We've only got two or three years left. We've got all of our survival food, so we're just gonna ride this thing out to the end."

Seriously?

Why do we have two or three years left? Where does it say that in the Bible? Where are these misled people getting their math?

Understand that when a person speaks this way, he or she is robbing others around them of hope and ushering them into a helpless, disheartened, ineffective, escape-ism mentality. People who are resigned to wait something out, holed up in their bunker filled with ammo and emergency food, are no longer in the fight. They are less than spectators, waiting for the inevitable—the unavoidable—to *happen already*. Now, not only are these folks *not* aiding God's army, but they are effectively assisting the armies of the enemy by shutting other soldiers down.

Choose this day whom you will serve!

Be careful who you listen to—and whose words you repeat to others. Between YouTube, Facebook, Twitter, other corrupt news sources all over the world, and churches or denominations with opposing views and clashing doctrines, it can get tough to discern which voices come from whom sometimes, and which of these voices are of trustworthy report. Keep it simple. Listen for *God's* voice.

My prayer is, "I just want You Lord. I want to do Your will. I don't care about the rest of it."

I often tell people that I don't worry about when the Lord will come back. And I really don't. When we start worrying about when the Lord is coming back, *that, too*, becomes an obstacle. When He does come back—if our hearts are right—it doesn't matter what the timeline is.

All we need to care about is the mission while we're still here. And what is the mission?

Take ground, and hold that ground for the kingdom of God at all costs! Win souls for Christ! Don't focus on the obstacles or the storms!

God Is Merciful, But He Does Have a Timeline

Don't get me wrong. Just because I say that we are not at the Great Tribulation and that we are not headed for certain doom, make no mistake: God has *had it* with corruption. As I said before, He is getting ready to clean house! He is fed up with it in our government, our judicial system, our churches…everywhere. He has told me that He will be removing people from their stations and bringing in new people who will act honorably with their newfound posts.

God is establishing His government upon the earth right now. And this is where the remnant is going to come in. We're going to see an emergence of apostles, prophets, preachers, and evangelists, all from within the remnant, come forth and be a part of the restructuring that's about to take place. These will be people who have been hidden in the crowds of lackluster churchgoers, whose job it will be to move into these new roles as they become vacant and as new people are *called*.

We have people behind the pulpit right now who have no business being there, because they should be in the marketplace, and we have people in the marketplace who should be behind the pulpit. We have people calling themselves prophets who aren't; we have people calling themselves pastors who should not be. Soon, and *very* soon, God is going to bring order to all of that. He will remove people who don't belong where they are and shuffle people around. We need to be ready for a period fraught with transition.

There will also be a lot of job openings in Washington. People who are in the Army of God, members of the remnant, will be called to be senators, congressmen, and judges. And that's only the beginning. God will place these new soldiers in the correct positions, and they will begin to legislate according to the Constitution, the Bible, and Christian standards. The rest of us are called to be involved, supportive, and vocal, and to pray for these people.

In November of 2015, God gave me a word I call "Time Is Up for Those Who Are Corrupt." This will be elaborated upon in the next chapter, but understand that God is finished letting the enemy play "king of the hill" on His playground.

chapter six

America, America

America! America! God shed His grace on thee,
And crown thy good with brotherhood
From sea to shining sea!
KATHARINE LEE BATES, "America, the Beautiful"[5]

America has had a special blessing on her since the beginning. God has protected and made her prosperous since her origin. Since the foundation, many lives have been lost defending the freedom that you and I enjoy each day. Sadly, however, like many generations of people in the Bible who were blessed by God, America has had her share of rebelliousness. While this could very easily be its own book, elaboration is not necessary—as no observer today has to look far to see the traces of this rebellion rampant throughout our entire society.

Often, people who operate under a legalistic spirit are quick to call down God's wrath upon America for the sin that they perceive exists within American society. Vitally important, yet forgotten, are the seeds that America has sown that go unmentioned by these same critics.

America has, since the beginning, been a force for good within the modern world. This is a fact rarely acknowledged by our modern cynics. As humans, we sometimes get so hung up on burning America for her sins that we don't remember the sacrifices America has made for the good of others.

Let's be very clear: Under no circumstances has America been the "nation of innocent angels," and absolutely no one on earth can ever earn God's favor by deeds:

> *What then? are we better than they? No, in no wise: for we have*
> *before proved both Jews and Gentiles, that they are all under sin;*
> *As it is written, There is one righteous, no, not one.*
> ROMANS 3:9–10

God did however, reveal to me that He still loves America and has chosen her not only for a good work, but to be restored to the blessings of her youth. In October of 2015, God gave me the following prophecy titled "America, America":

The Spirit of God says, "America, America, oh how I love thee! America, America, oh how I have chosen thee! For as England was to the D-Day invasion, so shall America be for My end-time harvest. For England was the Headquarters, the hub from which the D-Day assault was launched, so shall it be for My America for the end-time harvest. For as England had men, women, equipment, food, money, weapons, and supplies of all kinds which poured in from all over the world, so shall all these things pour into My chosen America.

"America, I have chosen you as the launching platform for the worldwide assault on the spiritually oppressed peoples of the earth. People will say, 'How are we chosen? It's as if America's frozen.' Am I not the God of the universe and all of creation? I have heard the cries of My people that have sought My face, and I WILL HEAL THEIR NATION! People will ask how I will do this. I shall do this in two parts."

First: The Spirit of God says, "Army of God, out of the darkness! I COMMAND YOU TO ARISE AND TAKE YOUR PLACE! For I have given you extra time, mercy, and grace. Go, Go, Go! Do not slow down. Begin to take and hold your ground, for there is no more time to waste. America will once again be in the great light. The enemy will say, 'Oh, the light, the light! It shines so bright! There is nothing else left to do but take flight!' And indeed they will. The sign will be a mass exodus in the natural as the spiritual flee."

Second: The Spirit of God says, "The gatekeeper, the gatekeeper, the President of the United States is the spiritual gatekeeper. I have chosen this man Donald Trump and anointed him as President for such a time as this. Can you not see this? For even in his name, Donald—meaning world leader (spiritual connotation; faithful); Trump—meaning to get the better of, or to outrank or defeat someone or something often in a highly public way.

"This man I have chosen will be a faithful world leader, and together with My army, will defeat all of America's enemies in the spiritual and in the natural. You will see it manifest before your eyes. I will use this man to shut gates, doors, and portals that this past president has opened. He will open gates, doors, and portals that this past president has shut. My Army shall not be silenced; they will begin to see he is the one I have chosen. They will begin to rally around him and keep him covered in spiritual support, and as you gain ground they will say America is not frozen."

God has chosen America to be the hub for the end-time harvest. This means that by promise of supplies, men, women, and workforce, resources will begin to flow into America again. Our economy will become stronger and jobs will begin to return to our country. Spiritual growth will flourish and morale will lift. Leaders will start to legislate according to the values of the Bible, and national security will return to where it should be.

Not only will the blessing of God on our land return economically, it will return *spiritually* as well. We will be empowered to reach the spiritually oppressed people of the earth. God has heard the cries of His people, and has promised to heal our land.

> *If my people, which are called by my name,*
> *shall humble themselves, and pray, and seek my face,*
> *and turn from their wicked ways; then will I hear from heaven,*
> *and will forgive their sin, and will heal their land.*
> 2 CHRONICLES 7:14

The 2016 Election Was Only the Beginning

Donald Trump was chosen as God's anointed, as I have said so many times thus far, for such a time as this. But really, what is so special about him? Only that God has appointed him to perform a role at this time, and he has answered that call. He is actually just an ordinary man, like anyone else. After all, that's all any of us really are: ordinary people who do extraordinary things when we surrender to the will of God.

It's time for people to remember the seeds that America has sowed. Christians aren't as outnumbered and powerless as they have been led to believe, so it's important to stop buying into a defeatist mentality. God is changing our country's government radically. It will be a fight, but we are under new administration, and the judicial system is heading for an overhaul as well. Prayer and revival from the baseline level of our culture will mean changes from the top down, and these changes will trickle like a waterfall that floods everything.

Don't be afraid as you watch transition within our government. Remember that God has overcome the world and all that is in it. He has told me that He is designing a dream team to lead our country's future. Understand that the indications marked in these following prophecies are signs and reminders of the hope that God is in control and our Redeemer lives!

The Right to Bear Arms

A word the Holy Spirit revealed to me on October 13, 2015, called "Don't be Deceived, Get in the Fight!" states:

> The Spirit of God says, "Beware, beware, the enemy roams about seeking whom he can devour and this sitting President is doing just that in this hour. He's full of lies and deceit and is very hateful; he spreads division and corruption with every mouthful. Beware when he says, 'Look over here, what the right hand is doing,' to divert your attention from what the left hand is doing, is his intention. This is a setup from this President and his minions, from the hate, the division, and Hillary Clinton. Why can no one see this? For the signs are clear to see, that this President and his minions shall try for three. A sign will be, he will try and take the guns so the people can't rise up and stop him when he tries to run. He will not succeed, for this is the peoples' right, but make no mistake, it will be a fight."

It's called "prestidigitation" (which is the origin of that old-school term "Presto!" in vintage magic shows) or "sleight of hand," and it's the oldest trick in the book. A magician calls the crowd's attention to one hand in preparation of performing a trick (does anyone recall that white-gloved hand wiggling fingers above the bouquet or handkerchief?), while the other hand—that hand nobody is watching—moves about quickly to execute the illusion. Many successful magicians have "wowed" audiences with this technique.

We have watched this prophecy unfold throughout the 2016 election. And what a fight it has been! Some were claiming that Clinton would take all the guns from U.S. citizens, while others said that was a completely fallacious rumor. Some claimed that the issue was just an impassioned debate about whether to tighten gun control laws. Others vowed boldly that their guns would likely be pried from their cold, stiff, lifeless fingers.

Consider again that age-old psychological phenomenon of prestidigitation in relation to the whole firearms issue. People were so caught up worrying about their guns being literally removed from their hands that they almost missed the real issue. Watch the one hand, while the other one makes your Second Amendment rights disappear. An important part of the backstory on this is as follows: "In 1996, Martin Bryant entered a café at the site of a historic penal colony at Port Arthur, Tasmania. The 28-year-old ate lunch before pulling a semi-automatic rifle from his bag and embarking on a killing spree. By the time he was apprehended the next morning, 35 people were dead and 23 had been wounded. Bryant had become the worst mass-murderer in Australia's history."[6]

After this event, Australia changed its gun laws, rendering many guns illegal to own and offering a one-year buyback for them at fair market value. After the one-year "grace period" expired, penalties for continuing to possess these firearms became enforceable. By initiating this law, citizens were *mandatorily* required to sell their guns back to their government. Because the premise of the buyback in the first place was the now-illegal status of these weapons, gun owners were not allowed to replace them with identical guns. Granted, some argue that Australian citizens are still allowed to own *certain* firearms, but they are extremely limited and cannot be purchased without a valid, "approved" reason. Guns are now virtually impossible to obtain legally in Australia.

Many Clinton supporters defended the Australian government's way of confiscating firearms, again, citing a mere increase on gun precautions. Clinton has snuggled right into their sympathies, emphasizing intentions of making a safer place for our citizens. (Ironic, when one considers the breach in national security she has not yet been indicted for.) When asked about her intentions toward gun ownership rights, Clinton stated:

"In the Australian example, as I recall, that was a buyback program," she said. "The Australian government, as part of trying to clamp down on the availability of automatic weapons, offered a good price for buying hundreds of thousands of guns and then they basically clamped down going forward in terms of, you know, more of a background check, more of a permitting approach.

"But they believed, and I think the evidence supports them, that by offering to buy back those guns they were able to, you know, curtail the supply and set a different standard for gun purchases in the future.

"Now (U.S.) communities have done that; communities have done gun buyback programs. But I think it would be worth considering doing that on the national level if that could be arranged."[7]

Impressive in this case is that even *Fox News* reporter John R. Lott expressed concern about the varying methods Clinton might use to remove guns from the homes in America: "From changing the Supreme Court to make it possible to again ban guns in the United States to making it more costly to own guns, I predict that a President Hillary Clinton will do four things to either ban guns or at least reduce gun ownership, especially for poor people."[8]

He then went on to describe his concerns. In a nutshell, these concerns are summed up by way of observing that what cannot be worked around through changing actual constitutional law can be solved by heaping up a pile of fees so high that, in this country currently riddled with economically struggling households, gun ownership would become largely a thing of the past.

When asked if she supported a citizen's right to own guns, Clinton would not directly answer. She just said, "If it's a constitutional right." But everyone is aware that if given the opportunity, she would appoint Supreme Court judges who would reinforce gun bans.

Additionally, she supported a 25 percent sales tax on handguns in 1993. This is an astronomical amount to add to an already expensive purchase. I suppose the method here accomplishes something to the tune of this: "If you can't beat 'em, starve 'em out!"

Outrageously expensive additional costs could be incurred pre-screening gun purchases, at this point adding as much as $125 additional dollars to the price of a gun—and that could increase if fees are raised subsequently. When asked about this, her only answer was that gun violence costs us all a lot of money. (It didn't seem to matter that guns help *stop* crime as well.)

She has alluded to support for the idea of holding gun makers and sellers responsible for the crimes committed with guns. This will also cause prices to go up and supply to become more limited.

So, in light of this heated debate that was such a focal point of the 2016 election, was Hillary Clinton threatening to come to your house in a black helicopter and forcefully take your guns? Not necessarily.

However, if attempts to tamper with the Second Amendment were not successful in the one hand, then be wary: There is always the trick the other hand is getting ready to pull. Imagine this scenario: The majority of guns have been proclaimed illegal, and you have been required by law (with threat of impending penalties) to sell the ones you currently own. New ones are of limited supply and prohibitively expensive to acquire, due to manufacturers becoming strained and liability-shy. Permits and screening processes have become expensive, time-consuming, bureaucratic-red-tape hurdles—the likes of which even an Olympic medalist could not leap across. On top of this, the multiple, outlandish fees tagged onto the end of the purchase now add possibly several hundred extra dollars on top of the item's retail price. Pile onto this 25 percent taxation on the purchase.

Now ask yourself: How many households in this economically depressed nation could afford to replace their guns? Understand that by Clinton's own words, she would have "curtail[ed] the supply and set a different standard for gun purchases in the future" had she been given the chance.

This was a victory for citizens who believe in the Second Amendment.

That is the thing about tricky politicians. They can hold their agenda in their hand right in front of you, and when you point at it and reveal it for all to see, they move their hand ever so subtly, expose an empty palm, and say, "Who, me?"

Fulfillment of Prophecies Underway

Earlier I shared with you the beginning of the "America, America" prophecy. The rest is as follows:

[The Spirit of God says,] "The seeds, the seeds, why is no one asking about the seeds? What about all the seeds America has sown since her birth? America has never received her harvest. For I will use President Trump and My Army to bring back to America all that she has sown. This will be used for My harvest. America will prosper like never before in her history as a nation. All of the financial seeds you have sown around the world: food, clothing, 90 percent of My Gospel that has gone throughout the earth, has come from My chosen America. Her blood has been spilled on foreign soil to free the oppressed so that My Gospel could go forward. America, your harvest is here! It shall parallel with your spiritual harvest in the natural, so do not fear."

The Spirit of God says, "The border, the border is a 2,000 mile gate, that's flowing across with demonic hate. I will use my President to shut this gate and seal it shut. It must be shut. Then I will use him and My Army to root out evil structures that are still there, to the point that the government will begin to call on My Army. They will prophetically locate these structures so they may be dismantled before any evil can take place.

"OPEC, OPEC, take a hike; for I am tired of your evil energy spikes. When My President wakes office you will shake and quake, you will say, "America no longer needs us," and that is true, for she will be energy independent for the red, white, and blue. For a sign will be given when prices go low, for a gallon of gas will be one dollar and below."

The Spirit of God says, "The Supreme Court shall lose three, and My President shall pick new ones directly from MY TREE!

"Are you still not convinced that he's My anointed, and that he's the one I have appointed? Why can no one figure it out, the news media, the people, and the so-called wise? Why, when he's attacked, do his poll numbers rise? Those who attack him, their numbers go low, even to the point of a big, fat zero. It's simple to see, this man I have appointed, for in My word, is your answer. I said, 'Do not touch my anointed, especially my prophets.' If you are still not convinced about what My word says, another sign will be given. It will be a WARNING TO ALL, especially those who will NOT LISTEN."

The Spirit of God says, "The sign will be El-Chapo, El-Chapo, your evil reign has come to an end. Who do you think you are, attacking my anointed? Turn yourself in and repent and I will spare you. If you do not, you and those that follow you will surely die a very public death for the entire world to see. For no one touches my anointed. I the Lord am an all-seeing and all-knowing God. I will be the one to disclose your location; the den, the den that you and your vipers hide in. For time is short and the spirit of death is at your door, and the world will see your dead body, and the red shirt you wore."

The Unlikely Candidate

I have said before that we are about to harvest the seeds that America has planted since her origin. The prophecy above says toward the end: "Why, when he's attacked, do his poll numbers rise?"

Many did not think that Trump could win the election. Such an unusual turn of events has rarely happened in American history. Perhaps the director of the movie *Hillary's America*, Dinesh D'Souza, summed it up best when he said:

The experience of elation that I felt on Tuesday with Trump's election has not in any way subsided. No. And let us pause to reflect on the momentousness of that accomplishment. No man has gone to the White House not coming from elected office since Eisenhower, and Eisenhower was the Supreme Commander of World War II. So what Trump has done on Tuesday is unprecedented. And in some ways no one else could have pulled that off. I'm trying to describe the feeling that I had in seeing those election results, and I think the best analogy I can think of is it was kind of a prison break feeling, kind of the experience that we saw in the Shawshank Redemption of breaking out of captivity.[9]

But although this is an unusual turn of events in American history, it is nothing new to God. He has often brought the unlikely candidate into a place of honor and set him charge over important things. Think of David, the little shepherd boy who defeated Goliath and went on to reign as king. Or Gideon, the least of his household in the smallest clan of Manasseh, whose meager army of three hundred defeated the army of thousands of Midianites. God has told us that in our weakness, He is strong. He will fight our battles. He will bring the people into place from the most unlikely places to show off His power and bring His own glory.

Since Trump's election, the economy has already shown improvement. Before he had even taken office, investors were looking at potential positives, the stock market had hit new all-time highs, and the Dow Jones broke records by closing high thirteen out the twenty-one days following the election. God has told me that He will be bringing America back to prosperity. America will thrive economically, spiritually, physically, and will be positively regarded in foreign policy again.

———

UPDATE: Taylor's Prophetic Words Are Beginning to Come True
While many in the media seem to love-to-hate President Trump, it cannot be denied that his accomplishments speak for themselves. After all, his propensity for victory would stymy even those who dislike him on a personal level. Furthermore, regardless of a person's political stance on the ethics and morals which back actions taken by Trump, no one would deny that the man is tenacious about keeping his promises. Paul Bedard, of *The Washington Examiner*, stated in his article reflecting on Trump's accomplishments over his first two years in office: "The Trump administration's often overlooked list of achievements has surpassed those of

former President Ronald Reagan at this time and more than doubled since the last tally of accomplishments after his first year in office, giving President Trump a solid platform to run for re-election on."[10]

Beyond this, as it pertains to Trump's ability to deliver on future undertakings that were foundational assurances during his election, 2016 Trump campaign pollster John McLaughlin was quoted: "They told him [Trump] he couldn't be president and beat the establishment and he did. For two years the establishment is telling him he can't do things in Washington and he's succeeding in spite of them. He never retreats. He doesn't back up. He's relentless. He just wins."[11]

While this "winning" may come as a surprise to those who opposed Donald Trump, these celebrated (or *not* so celebrated) successes are only the beginning. Mark Taylor outlined these elements through his prophecies written years ago, and the current revolution within this nation's political climate is certainly of no surprise to him. In fact, recall that Mark's message from the Lord indicated that America was headed for a time of "cleaning house," a time of revival, and that she would begin to harvest the seeds that she has sown—throughout the entire world—over a span of many, *many* decades. This fruition is about to begin, but in order for these events to launch, our country's government must rearrange, making room for the Almighty. As godly men and women are appointed to serve within these ranks, obviously there are those of ulterior agenda who wish to obstruct this movement. Mark reminds us to be continually in prayer for our president; he has a fight on his hands at this moment. However, his winning streak paints a picture of hope for this country, and thus, the world. Make no mistake, however, President Trump, as Mark Taylor reminds us, is only a man. Any triumph for the kingdom of heaven gained under his watch is only an act of the Lord God Almighty, as imbued through the human conduit of the Lord's anointed. As we engage in prayer and supplication for our president, we likewise fortify the battle for good which takes place in the spiritual realm over America every day.

———

The Border

In moving ahead with promises made during his campaign, Trump has wasted no time in taking direct, affirmative action. In a recent news release, we read: "President Donald Trump on Wednesday started to reshape U.S. immigration enforcement policies via executive action, taking his first steps toward fulfilling some of the most contentious pledges that defined his campaign—building a border wall and speeding the deportation of undocumented immigrants."[12]

His plans of restoring America to prosperity include creating a wall along the southern border of the country and requiring that Mexico pays the bill. As our neighboring country has rejected this idea, Trump plans to begin negotiations with the Mexican government in the upcoming months. Trump maintains that a firm boundary between the two countries will strengthen each country individually, as well as decrease crime in America and keep migrants from cutting through Mexico as they travel northward from locations farther south. Our economy will be strengthened when the number of undocumented immigrants is lessened as well. Further, the release reveals: "'Beginning today, the United States of America gets back control of its borders,' Trump told employees of the Department of Homeland Security at the department's headquarters in Washington."[13]

Although met with some staunch adversity, Trump claims that he can work within the parameters of the existing system and laws, and has ordered that planning sessions for this project begin immediately. Construction of the actual wall will commence months from the time of this writing. This prophecy is in the stages of fulfillment now: "The sign will be a mass exodus in the natural as the spiritual flee," as the departure of illegals leaving the country is a sign that the Army of God is advancing in the spiritual realm.

As I write this, Trump has recently ordered increases totaling an additional five thousand agents as well as ten thousand new Immigration and Customs enforcement officers to follow through with deportations of undocumented immigrants, starting with those who have been so much as charged with a crime in the U.S. (Obama's policy was much more lenient, prioritizing only those convicted of felonies or serious or multiple misdemeanors.) Closely following these will be undocumented immigrants who have abused public benefits or are simply somehow considered a risk to public safety or national security as determined by an immigration officer.

As for notorious criminals who have haunted the territories of the American border, increasing crime, violence, and drug inflow to the U.S., they will be captured and prosecuted in the same way as El Chapo—who has an important decision to make. God has said, "Turn yourself in and repent and I will spare you. If you do not, you and those that follow you will surely die a very public death for the entire world to see." This prophecy is underway, but not finished. God is merciful and not willing that any should suffer, so even in this prophetic word, He has given this man an opportunity to change his fate.

———

UPDATE: International Relations and National Security

Mark Taylor's prophetic words stated that President Trump would be a faithful world leader, and would fight to defeat America's domestic and international enemies, in both spiritual and natural matters. Similarly, Taylor's words assured that this president would close gates and portals opened by former administrations, as well as opening those closed previously. Taylor relayed God's message that as U.S. leadership began to legislate according to righteous value, national security would gradually return to its proper condition.

President Trump's proactive management of the U.S.' international relations can be seen by his willingness to draw hard lines where he feels they are in America's best interest. From his pursuit of the Wall bordering between the States and Mexico, to the handling of international nuclear treaties, Trump has made his position extremely clear: "Under my [Trump's] administration, we will never apologize for advancing America's interests."[14] When President Trump announced in a State of the Union Address in early 2019 that America would be withdrawing from the INF (Intermediate-range Nuclear Forces) treaty due to Russia's continuing violation of the terms within the agreement, he was met with a standing ovation.

The leader has also declared that, when national security is challenged, America will "out-spend and out-innovate all others by far."[15] Trump reports that he is willing to renegotiate a new nuclear agreement with Russia, which would possibly include the addition of new countries to the treaty, if terms are fair and followed. Similarly, the president continues nuclear summits with North Korean leader Kim Jong Un, which are proceeding even as these pages are printed. He likewise pushes for more funding toward military and missile defense programs that will endeavor to counter the threat of such weapons posed by North Korea.[16]

The president fortified the war on terrorism by reversing his predecessor's order to shut down Guantánamo Bay, stating that such a move would show a sign of weakness on behalf of the war on terrorism.[17] Of this matter, Trump stated: "I am asking Congress to ensure that in the fight against ISIS and al-Qa'ida, we continue to have all the necessary power to detain terrorists—wherever we chase them down, wherever we find them, and in many cases for them it will now be Guantánamo Bay."[18]

The president has additionally increased national security by instituting a travel ban which restricts immigration from Muslim countries; a move backed by the Supreme Court.[19] Chief Justice John Roberts commented that the Court found this order to be well within presidential authority, and was "expressly premised on legitimate purposes: preventing entry of nationals who cannot be adequately vetted and inducing other nations to improve their practices."[20] Despite rumors that the ban was the result of religious prejudice, Roberts stated that the language contained therein provided no substance backing this notion, adding:

"The text says nothing about religion."[21] In addition to these preventative maneuvers, Trump's administration has dramatically slowed the influx of refugees entering the country through increased screening in an effort to fortify national security.[22]

In Mark Taylor's prophetic word, he addresses the 2,000-mile border by calling it "a gate flowing with demonic hate." According to this message, Trump will close this access and seal it. Once this has occurred, evil will be rooted out by both combined and separate efforts made by the American government and God's army.

During his presidential campaign, Trump announced that he would build a wall between the States and Mexico, and he would make Mexico pay the bill for this undertaking. As of early 2019, official construction of the wall looms in the very near future, as Trump vigilantly continues to fight for construction of the wall by beginning to secure contractors.[23] Funding has been no small obstacle, but the president presses ahead toward this massive task which will feature such precautions as "detection technology, lighting, video surveillance, and an all-weather patrol road parallel to the levee wall,"[24] along with 18-foot-tall steel bollards attached to the top,[25] and 150 feet of vegetation removal along the enforcement zones.[26] Adding to the buzz of construction-related momentum is the fact that currently a 4-mile long segment of wall in El Paso, Texas is underway, "bringing President Donald Trump one step closer to seeing construction of his long-promised border wall between the U.S. and Mexico."[27] Construction is officially set to begin at the time of this writing, in February 2019.

The president's initiative toward victory over both domestic and international threat runs deeper than that of a physical wall, as can be seen by his establishing of crime reducing task forces who work within communities to increase safety. He has even signed an executive order which concentrates more resources toward fighting transnational criminal organizations,[28] stating desired elimination of "gangs and cartels who flood our streets with drugs and violence."[29] Trump likewise signed legislation empowering authorities against websites which enable sex trafficking and prostitution, and increasing penalties to individuals facili-tating such conduct.[30] In addition to this, the president has created a task force which works toward the prosecution of human traffickers.[31]

Mark Taylor's message called out El Chapo, telling him that his evil reign would come to an end. According to Mark, God gave the notorious criminal the following ultimatum: Turn yourself in and you will be spared; otherwise you will suffer a public death that all the world will see. The infamous criminal, Joaquín "El Chapo" Guzmán, is stated to be "argu-ably the most powerful drug dealer in the history of the trade."[32] Previ-ously, Guzmán had both evaded arrest and escaped incarceration, but in January of 2016, the man was finally captured and, as of early 2019, faces trial for indictments including importing and distributing narcotics, conspiracy to commit murder, continuing criminal enterprise, firearm vio-lations pertaining to drug trafficking, and money laundering.[33] Even as I write this, the jury is deliberating the trial of El Chapo as it pertains to 10 federal charges.[34] Conditions of the kingpin's extradition from Mexico guarantee that the U.S. federal court will not seek the death penalty in this case.[35] However, if found guilty, Guzmán stands to spend the rest of his life in a maximum security prison facility.[36]

On a domestic level, Trump's administration has taken the initiative to fight the modern opioid crisis by raising awareness within communities and making resources available to those who wish to fight their addic-tion. Since he took office, "we have seen a 264 percent increase in the prescribing of naloxone"[37] —a synthetic drug which blocks the nervous system's opiate receptors—and also a "16 percent increase in the pre-scribing of one form of addiction treatment."[38] Likewise, the president has fought to raise awareness by erecting a temporary memorial on the Ellipse of the President's Park near the White House, entitled "Prescribed to Death,"[39] wherein victims claimed by the opioid epidemic were remem-bered. In addition, Trump has presented common ground with leadership of other countries by requesting that world leaders unite to combat drug addiction.[40]

———

OPEC and the Energy-Independent America

The short prophetic word "Energy, Energy" penned on December 16, 2016, reads:

> The Spirit of God says, "Energy, Energy, I am releasing new energy. For this new energy that I am releasing will make My America and My Israel energy independent. For America and Israel will now be the top energy producers in the world. This new energy and the technology to capture it will spring forth from the depths as the volcano erupts from the depths. This is the sign that will be given…a massive volcanic eruption will signal that this is the time for My America and Israel and the end of the energy corruption. OPEC, your evil regime will no longer be tolerated. You will no longer be needed, for you refuse to listen to My words and have not heeded. For when that ring of fire blows its top, it will be a sign to you that you will lose your stock and the covenant you have with that ring will be lost."
>
> The Spirit of God says, "You countries that have dominated energy for decades, to move your evil agenda, are charged with this guilt. Your days are numbered and you will say, 'Look how fast this was built.' My America and Israel will be one and because of this, you will be undone. Because of your rage, and the money you made from those countries you manipulated and attacked from within, you will now have to turn to those countries for help on a whim. For your wells will go dry and your finances too, for you will now be fed from the Red, White, and Blue."

Have you noticed that you are paying less for oil products in these last few years? It is because we are currently watching this prophecy unfold. The Organization of the Petroleum Exporting Countries, or OPEC, is basically a cooperative board of thirteen nations who, together, since the 1960s, have regulated the production and costs of oil products on a global level. As American shale oil production picks up, demand for OPEC's yields is beginning to drop. Between the years 2011 and 2013 alone the production within the U.S. increased by 50 percent. Because of this increased local availability, prices have continued to plummet. Being such a large controller for up to 73 percent of the oil yields of the world (up until very recently), OPEC normally would have stepped in, slowing production to drive the price back up, stabilizing the market. But this time, OPEC has done no such thing. This has caused the market to let loose, much like an inflated, untied balloon released over a room filled with children.

Simultaneously, in all of this, many of those who had invested in petroleum products based upon expected prices—and backed by the false security that OPEC would regulate the pricing to protect their venture—have watched as their assets tanked, unprotected. Many drillers, who operate on borrowed money, now find that their incoming prices cannot support the high-yield debt they regularly use to finance their operations. By not intervening, OPEC has attempted to snuff out much of their competition. For some of these competing producers, this tactic has been successful at forcing them to a halt. OPEC's strategy has been to reduce competition, then come back in, regain control, and raise prices again. Ironically, Russia and America are now producing their own shale oil products and do not exist within the controlling clenches of OPEC.

During the 2016 election, Clinton tried at one point to state that America was energy independent. This is not true, yet. The prophecy is still unfolding. One-quarter of our oil products are still imported. She would love to lead the population to believe that we have arrived, that we *could* arrive, on our own, without God's help. But this will not happen without the Lord's blessing or providence.

Donald Trump has asserted that he has a plan to bring America to energy independence. Some skeptics may doubt his ability to pull this one off, but recall the other changes that we have discussed so far in this chapter that are already beginning to occur, and as I write this, he has been in the office barely two months. A recent report of his plan comes from Business Insider: "This includes developing new oil fields in the U.S., creating 'at least half a million new jobs' in energy, and promoting natural gas over coal in order to tackle emissions. Also on the list are making 'America energy independent' and the aim for it to be 'totally independent of any need to import energy from the OPEC cartel or any nations hostile to our interest.'"[41]

America will become more energy efficient in the future. The Lord has told me that OPEC will say, "America no longer needs us," and as the prophecy says immediately following this, "that is true, for she will be energy independent for the red, white, and blue. For a sign will be given when prices go low, for a gallon of gas will be one dollar and below."

Because so much of Russia's economy is dependent on oil, the decrease in profitability for the petroleum market has hurt them. They were already economically endangered due to the previous political climate in their region. This sets the scene for the prophecies to be fulfilled between America and Russia in the near future. We are on some levels in the same boat as each other now, and are gaining common ground within our circumstances as nations. As America's border situation strengthens and its international esteem rises, simultaneous with Russia's need for economic boosting and a newfound camaraderie as outsiders on the OPEC situation, the two entities at this moment are positioning toward beginning the fulfillment of the prophecies regarding America's relationship with Russia.

———

UPDATE: America Makes Strides toward Energy Independence
Mark Taylor's prophetic word stated that in the future, OPEC would no longer be a provider for the U.S., as America will be energy independent. In

fact, Mark's bold statement goes so far as to say that America and Israel will be the top energy producers in the world, and the gas will be below one dollar per gallon again. While we have not seen the full fruition of these elements as of yet, we have definitely seen changes within America's ability to produce its own energy. A volatile volley (that began as early as 2011) continues to take place between President Trump and OPEC; the former continues to blame the latter for increased oil prices, stating that he will not tolerate market manipulation.[42] In turn, OPEC responds by threatening production cuts and inconsistency of supply prices.[43]

In the meantime, the U.S. etches its way closer to energy independence. President Trump continues to propagate energy production across the American continent. In fact, in December of 2018, for the first time in over 70 years, the U.S. exported more oil than it imported.[44] Up to now, Trump has maintained the position that rather than asserting alternative energies or energy scarcity, that the answer to America's energy crisis is found in energy development.[45] A recent article released by *Investor's Business Daily* stated that "advanced drilling technologies have opened vast expanses of domestic oil and natural gas. And as domestic production skyrocketed, imports have been steadily dropping."[46] Furthermore, the same source stated that Trump is aware that the key to energy independence is not found through energy plans or scarcity awareness, but rather "just requires government to get out of the way so that oil companies can get at the vast supplies of good old oil and gas right under U.S. soil."[47]

It would certainly appear that the statement is true, as Trump has had no issue with tapping American resources in an effort to rebuild industry and become energy independent. While some would encourage him to take a more environmental approach, president Trump has made it clear that his priority is American economic and industrial recovery and energy independence. And, while the man's tactics may bring him as many adversaries as it does friends, he is certainly making headway on his goals. By July 2017, U.S. coal exports had jumped by 61 percent, while Trump overthrew existing environmental policies to help revive the coal-mining industry, which had been withering.[48] Simultaneously, Trump actively pursues his plans to make America more energy self-sufficient through his launching of a draft proposal to drill the Arctic National Wildlife Refuge (ANWR).[49]

In a similar strain, President Trump reversed Obama's blockade of the Keystone XL pipeline, allowing crude oil to be streamed from Canada to refineries on the Gulf Coast,[50] which will be capable of transporting "approximately 1.1 million barrels of crude oil daily, non-stop from Alberta, Canada to market hubs in the Midwest and Texas."[51] In addition to the energy independence this derives for the U.S., it likewise produces approximately 20,000 manufacturing and construction jobs, increasing personal income for American workers by $6.5 billion for the duration of construction.[52] On top of these benefits, tax dollars generated for state governments, local entities, and communities along the pipeline route could amount to as much as $700 million. President Trump similarly allowed the Dakota Access Pipeline, bringing similar benefits, to commence construction as well.[53] Moreover, America, for the first time in 60 years, is a neutral net gas exporter again, contributing to a narrowing of its "trade imbalance."[54]

Hand in hand with Trump's determination to aid the U.S.' ability to become energy independent was his willingness to withdraw from the Paris Climate Accord. President Trump's reasons for this maneuver were stated as the agreement being disadvantageous toward the U.S. economy,[55] while not imposing practical requirements on the world's leading polluters.[56] Trump has stated his willingness to revisit the agreement if terms are presented that he deems to do more justice to the U.S. than previously asserted negotiations.

————

A Sign to Watch For

Note the portion of the prophecy that stated the Lord's words: "This is the sign that will be given…a massive volcanic eruption will signal that this is the time for my America and Israel and the end of the energy corruption."

I don't know if this will be a physical volcano or if this, as we discussed earlier in this chapter, is a prophecy more metaphoric in nature, but be watching in the news for this occurrence. It will be the sign that OPEC will be defeated and that Israel and America will be the top energy producers in the world.

The SEEDS Are Ready for Harvest

In the last paragraph of "Don't Be Deceived, Get in the Fight!" God says, "Take the fight to the enemy and you will be victorious for all to see, and America will be loved once again, even by some that used to be her enemies."

God is constantly reminding us that He is in control. We are not forsaken, or forgotten. He will make us victorious; He has already begun to! Our best days are ahead!

As the Church, we're often too quick to buy into the enemy's lies when he says we are weak, outnumbered, and impotent. We know that the enemy is actually the father of lies, but somehow we fall for this one almost every time. We forget that for generations God's people have been humbling themselves, praying, and asking God for intervention. We see only what shows up around us in the physical realm—the news media, TV, issues within government, society on the street in general—and we lose sight of the most important truth: His people *have* been praying, and He *has* been hearing them.

Think about the people you've known throughout your life, both at home and in church. Surely you have known at least a few of these precious unsung heroes of spiritual warfare: the older ladies of the church who were the first anybody called when prayer was needed; the elderly gent whose idea of a successful fishing trip was not measured by the biggest catch but by the closeness he had with God while out on the lake; the humble pastor of that small country church who sang *The Old Rugged Cross* as though its lyrics were the last words he might ever utter.

We forget about these people. We are, again, like the D-Day soldiers, looking all around us at the fallen, unable to see the reinforcements over the waves. If we would really start to take inventory, we would realize that we have been surrounded by these people. God's people have been calling out to their Lord since the beginning of this country, and the time of our redemption approaches!

America is now poised to be absolutely central in the upcoming, worldwide revival of one billion souls and will soon thrive in the natural and spiritual realm like never before. Now, just to be clear, we have *not earned* this honor. As the song says, He has "shed his *grace* on thee." But He has been, all along, aware of these faithful saints, scores of whom have gone on and now abide with Him, and He is bringing to fruition the fulfillment of His promise.

The Bible says that every time even a small sparrow falls from the sky, the Lord takes notice. In that case, He has definitely seen the American blood that has been spilled on foreign soil for the freedom of many from evil. He is the God of the fatherless and the widow. So we know that He watched as the elderly woman sent her last five dollars to mission funds, just as the woman in the Bible gave her last two coins. He has seen the generosity of an aggrieved child from a broken home who gave his entire allowance to a Convoy of Hope donation center to help survivors of a natural disaster (these are real instances involving real people that I know).

Are we Americans spoiled? Sure. Corrupt? Some of us are. Godless? Take a look around. But, God has made a promise to us.

If my people…

And He has heard your cries and will heal your land. He is already beginning! Don't look at the pain around you and lose hope.

These things I have spoken unto you, that in me ye might have peace. In the world ye shall find tribulation: but be of good cheer; I have overcome the world.

JOHN 16:33

The troubles we face today are only the birthing pains toward a better tomorrow. Again, recall how He agreed to Abraham that He would spare the city if there were as many as ten righteous. God has heard our cries. Lift your eyes to the mountains, America! Your deliverance draws nigh!

———

UPDATE: America's Economy Recovers as the Harvest Draws Near
In Mark Taylor's prophecies, he stated that God had made certain promises of richness to America. Recall that Mark has asserted America is to be the hub for the end-time harvest, and that the seeds she has sewn throughout the world will reap prosperity in our land. Mark specified that America will stockpile resources for this yield, and that jobs will return to our marketplace. He assures us that God has seen the sacrifices made by saints on behalf of the Great Commission, and that the money, services, material supplies, and even bloodshed that have been spent toward this means are not forgotten by God. Reciprocally, God will return to America our financial *and* spiritual reward.

Since President Trump was sworn in on January 17, 2017, the economy has made a considerable recovery, just as Mark's prophetic words foretold. In a previously faltering monetary state, the American economics responded quickly to Trump's leadership, and a society that was ready for reprieve from financial strain has felt some much-needed relief.

During the past two years, over 4 million jobs have been created in the American workforce.[57] The manufacturing market continues to pick up momentum, and is, in fact, at the fastest speed of increase that it has seen in three decades, totaling over 400,000 new manufacturing jobs added since Trump's election.[58] In addition to this, 95 percent of manufacturers are confident about the future, and thus continue to push for growth and expansion.[59] Retail economy has made a comeback, with Commerce Department figures showing that July of 2018 experienced retail sale increase of .5 percent, which was up 6.4 percent from July 2017,[60] and the Dow Jones Industrial Average, S&P 500, and NASDAQ have all hit record highs with the Dow reaching more record highs than has ever occurred during the same year before: 70 times in 2017.[61]

Furthermore, the U.S. has experienced a new anomaly: Since the dawn of America's birth, there are more jobs available than there are unemployed people. According to a *CNBC News* story in June of 2018, there are 6.7 million job openings in the U.S. and 6.4 million unemployed individuals.[62] This welcome dilemma brought about refreshing change for those concerned about finding work in our economic state, as March of 2018 was the first time the U.S. economy had faced such a conundrum.[63] In fact, many sources even report that more Americans are employed at this time than ever before,[64] although some debate this element and the final verdict is still out. However, there can be no doubt that for the first time in over 10 years, upcoming growth is anticipated at over 3 percent in the next calendar year,[65] in light of the 4.2 percent economic growth that occurred during the second quarter of 2018.[66]

In December of 2018, *Fox News* released a story that unemployment claims had hit a 49-year low while import prices decreased to their lowest point in more than three years.[67] Beyond this, African-Americans, Asian-Americans and Hispanic-Americans have achieved their lowest unem-ployment rate ever recorded.[68] But this growth is not limited to cultural background, as being without a job among youth is likewise lower than it has been for nearly 50 years, while joblessness for women is at the lowest rate it has been in 65 years.[69] Similarly, the same condition for Americans without a high school diploma is lower than has ever been recorded, while for veterans' this recently achieved its lowest rate in almost 20 years.[70]

Those benefiting from this are among American citizens of all classes. Median household income has achieved a post-recession high, increasing to $61,372 in 2017.[71] Nearly 3.9 million Americans have advanced off of the food stamp program since the 2016 election.[72] Furthermore, workers' employment lives are beginning to show more promise: Employers committed to train more than 4.2 million workers and students through the "Pledge to America's Workers"[73] program as a byproduct of the president's prioritization of vocational education in the workplace. Trump's administration has provided gross tax cuts totaling over $5.5 trillion, of which almost 60 percent of funds are anticipated to circulate back to families. Tax relief will likewise extend to specialized groups—such as small farmers—by increasing the standard deduction and the child tax credit.[74]

Employees are not the only laborers who will see financial improvement as a result of President Trump's actions. The changes that this national leader has brought about in tax laws provide significant financial relief for the small business owner. In fact, *The Hill's* Adam Brandon described him in June of 2018 by stating: "Trump is the most important small business leader the nation has seen in recent memory,"[75] reporting that The Small Business Optimism Index had hit its second high for the preceding 45 years.[76] This is in addition to the fact that consumer confidence is currently at an 18-year high.[77]

Simultaneously, self-employment is on the rise again, with 40 percent of Millennials voicing plans to quit traditional employment and start a small business.[78] Likewise, the results of current tax bill changes will now allow the small business to have the lowest top marginal tax rate they have seen in over 80 years.[79] As a result of these cuts, investments in the U.S. are soaring again, and $450 billion has already been recirculated into U.S. business economy, with more than $300 billion of this occurring in the first quarter of 2018.[80] This savings to companies as a byproduct of better tax advantages allows companies to pass such gains along to their employees: 9 out of 10 American workers are anticipated to see pay raises in the near future. This may sound like a pipe dream, but already "more than 6 million American workers have received wage increases, bonuses, and increase benefits thanks to tax cuts," while "over 100 utility companies have lowered electric, gas, or water rates thanks to the Tax Cuts and Jobs Act."[81]

Trump provided relief for individuals by making healthcare voluntary again, removing Obamacare's individual mandate penalty and simultaneously creating more affordable options via association/short-term duration plans. Medicare reforms continue to provide financial relief for seniors who now have more affordable medications available, in addition to helping to make more generic prescription drugs accessible as opposed to expensive, name-brand drugs. Furthermore, the president has signed the VA Choice Act and VA Accountability Act, and likewise expanded medical and mental health services to American veterans. The Right-To-Try legislation has provided possible means for terminally ill patients without hope to seek treatments for their illnesses by opting for experimental drug treatments, which will do two things: 1) offer the patient new hope for possible cure; 2) further scientific research backing possible new cures for terminal illnesses.[82]

Trump has likewise challenged government spending, and in an October 2018 meeting with his cabinet, requested that federal agencies cut back federal spending by 5 percent each for the fiscal year 2020.[83] Trump asked that NATO allies increase the amount they spent toward defense, relieving the U.S. from being the single entity which previously shouldered the greatest percentage of this cost.[84] In 2017, the U.S. spent over 3.5 percent of its GDP ($685 billion) on defense, while NATO members in Europe spent 1.46 percent ($249.7 billion).[85] President Trump has also stated that he would like to see these members bump their contributions up to 4 percent, but the current standing goal is an increase to 2 percent by the year 2024—an aim set back in 2014.[86]

The president has additionally amplified propensity for fair trade between the U.S. and China by imposing tariffs that begin at $50 billion and have the potential to escalate to $267 billion, thus encouraging this economic counterpart to deal more fairly with American companies.[87] The circumstances surrounding tariffs and the trade war engaged by Trump may seem to many as confusing, but Paul Davidson of *USA Today* simplifies these matters for us by clarifying: "Unlike other taxes, tariffs are less about raising revenue for governments and more about changing the flow of products across the borders and making foreign manufacturers' products more expensive for U.S. shoppers and businesses. That theoretically should help American companies that make competing products and are often undercut in price by foreign rivals."[88]

Trump's attempt to restore trade balance between neighboring countries also extended to imposing tariffs on such industries as steel and aluminum,[89] making successful strides toward renegotiating international trade between the U.S. and Canada and Mexico through announcing the USMCA's (U.S.-Mexico-Canada Agreement) replacement of NAFTA (North American Free Trade Agreement).[90]

chapter seven

———

Time Is Up for Those Who Are Corrupt

America! America! God mend thine ev'ry flaw,
Confirm thy soul in self-control,
Thy liberty in law!

KATHARINE LEE BATES, "America, the Beautiful"[91]

Total Governmental Transformation

In November of 2015, I wrote:

> The Spirit of God says, "I am neutering this sitting President, I am neutering this sitting President in this hour, so his evil and corrupt ideologies and theologies can no longer reproduce in this country I call MY UNITED STATES OF AMERICA! For this man who holds the title called the President of the United States, will begin to lose his grip from it and be stripped of it, for I the Lord God will rip it from him. This man who calls himself Commander in Chief, is nothing more than a lying deceitful Thief!"
>
> The Spirit of God says, "Time is up for those who are corrupt! For I shall begin to remove those who stand for evil in leadership and stand in the way of My agenda. Judges, Senators, Congressmen and women of all kinds, even in the local state,

and federal lines. Even the Supreme Court is not immune from their corrupt and evil ways, for I will remove some and expose their backdoor deals which have been at play. For My America has been chosen as the launching platform for My harvest, and she will be a light unto the world once again as I clean up that which is the darkest. Fear not America, your greatest days are ahead of you. Arise, My Army, and fight; and watch what I will do for you!"

The Clinton/Obama Machine

They strode on stage under the banner "Stronger Together." They held hands, arms raised up high, in a sign of unity. She wore a vibrant fuchsia jacket, he was in a white shirt, his sleeves rolled up. They were "fired up, ready to go." ready to make their case for a Clinton presidency, one that would build on the Obama legacy. (Kim Ghattas, *BBC News*[92])

It's been no secret that the same motor that turns the Clinton machine is the very one that turns the Obama machine. News media coverage made no effort whatsoever to hide the fact that Hillary Clinton's attempted presidency would be a continuation of the two terms that Obama had served. It was completely expected that after she had backed him so publicly in 2008, he would be right there behind her eight years later.

You may have heard the phrase, "Birds of a feather..." I don't even need to finish it. Likewise, I probably don't have to elaborate on how comparable these two candidates are. The fact that Obama would continue to stand behind such a blatantly corrupt candidate shows his own lack of interest in the well being of this country's future.

See what *Townhall News* had to say about Hillary Clinton at election time in 2016:

Indeed, a preponderance of legal and political analysts agree that the level of corruption and cover-up forcing Richard Nixon to resign his presidency in disgrace in 1974 pales by comparison to the evidence behind the multiple criminal investigations surrounding Hillary Clinton—the Democratic Party's embattled presidential nominee. Both the Clinton Foundation and Clinton email scandals represent, jointly and separately, Watergate on steroids.[93]

The 2016 election was a wild one, indeed. Who would ever have imagined that we would be, within the same sentence, talking about a person possibly becoming president of our country or going to prison? How is a person with such pending accusations even eligible to run for such a key role within our country's administration? That is how corrupt our government has become. The article just referenced goes on to share a quote from an earlier *Washington Times* article to assist in explaining how Obama's Department of Justice was actually a key player in keeping her indictment from occurring:

"Bret Baier, based on two sources, said in a tweet that 'barring obstruction they'd likely continue 2 push to try for an indictment.'" The "obstruction" reference, as Baier later explained, is presently being conducted by the Obama Department of Justice (DOJ) in general, and Attorney General Loretta Lynch in particular. As leaks indicate, the DOJ has placed a roadblock at every corner in an effort to obstruct the ongoing FBI investigations into Mrs. Clinton's illicit activities.[94]

This blatant, shameless corruption and tolerance of evil running rampant can be compared to the setting at the beach barracks that I referred to in the D-Day chapter, who were never expecting to be required to defend their location. These people have lived like there is no tomorrow, like their time of reign would be abundant, as though there were no judgment day for them. But as the Bible tells us, judgment day comes to us all.

The last paragraph in the "Commander-in-Chief Prophecy" says "...in this election they will spend billions to keep this president in; it will be like flushing their money down the toilet. Let them waste their money, for it comes from and it is being used by evil forces at work."

There's really no telling how much was actually spent trying to keep the Clinton/Obama machine in office. In trying to keep Trump out, they spent *train loads* of money. Literally billions. We'll never have an exact dollar count of how much was spent, but there is no question that between political groups, campaigning, Clinton's own money, and personal backers whose agenda toward the future of America was questionable, this prophecy was surpassed multiple times. Know this: Hillary Clinton had some very, *very* deep-pocketed supporters, many of whom were of dubious integrity and had anti-American principles in mind.

Some have doubted the authenticity of my word, because it said that this current president would try for another term. They immediately argue that Obama had the maximum amount of terms he *could* have, so, by default, they throw out the legitimacy of that word. Believe me when I say that Clinton and Obama are birds of a feather. Meaning: A Hillary Clinton presidential term would have been an Obama third term. It was, in both the natural and spiritual realms, a mere continuation of the same administration. The two are operating the same machine. Make no mistake about it!

That's where some people get tangled with the prophetic word. It doesn't always materialize the very way we think it's going to, because God's ways are not our ways, His thoughts are not our thoughts, and He does not limit His revelations based on our human concepts (Isaiah 55:8). Something can seem like it will be a literal manifestation in one method, and it can be something else entirely. It doesn't make the prophecy any less true; it's just different than our expectations. For example,

God could say, "A great bird will fall from the sky." That could be a literal, large bird falling from the sky—or it could mean that a plane crash is being foretold. So if you view Clinton as a continuation of Obama, as do I and *many* others in this country, then it means we narrowly escaped another four- to eight-year term of Obama-ism.

When I was participating in the live national prayer chain every morning just prior to the 2016 election, the Lord told me that we should be praying more *specifically*. I mean, after all, we had more than ten thousand people on the phone lines on any given day. Talk about "where two or more agree"! I decided to pray with target-focused repentance and intercession. I was to lead the prayer on 9/11. I thought about my prayer for two days before going on the line. I was surprised at how many prominent ministerial people had appeared on the call as guest prayer leaders already, yet I had heard no specific repentance of any kind, which I found unnerving and astonishing all at once.

So, I decided to take the lead. I repented for the 501(c)(3) and several other specific things instead of generally. While I was praying, I particularly asked the Lord to remove those in leadership who were corrupt. I didn't care if I was treading too harshly or offending anybody on the line. I just called it like I saw it. We hung up the phone at 9:17 a.m. on September 11, 2016. Within minutes, Hillary Clinton had collapsed after an early exit from a 9/11 memorial service for the entire world to see.

What is the significance of that? Well, as stated, *I asked with target-focused repentance and prayer for the Lord to remove those who were corrupt in leadership*—and that's precisely what happened. When she collapsed, that was a sign that the Clinton machine and anything attached to it was going to collapse. She lost her shoe when she fell, which means that entire lineup is going to lose their peace, which they since have begun to. (In dream interpretations, shoes are frequently a sign of peace. Additionally, according to Paul's Armor-of-God lineup in Ephesians 6, our feet are to be "fitted with the readiness that comes from the gospel of peace" [verse 15], which is indicative of both peace and a mission our feet will carry us toward [spreading the Gospel, for example]. As such, the symbolism behind Clinton's losing a shoe suggests that the peace that carried her into the mission of America's corruption has been removed.)

Am I saying that I am responsible for this event? Absolutely not! But I do believe in the power of target-focused prayer and repentance with thousands in unity and agreement. I believe that God was showing us that, together with specific, honed-in prayer, nothing is impossible for us!

When Obama was in office, those in the Clinton/Obama camp held the confidence. Now, that shoe has landed on the other foot. We are the ones gaining peace, because we are beginning to see desired changes.

In a prophetic word the Holy Spirit gave me on October 13, 2015 (mentioned briefly earlier), entitled "Don't be Deceived, Get in the Fight!" I wrote:

> The Spirit of God says, "The Clintons, the Clintons, your time has come to an end, for you both are being omitted for the crimes you have committed. Hillary's is no great secret and they will be her downfall, but Bill's will be exposed one after the other and it will be a windfall. For this time, you will not escape prosecution and restitution for the rape and prostitution. You thought no one saw, but I the Lord see it all, and now this will be your downfall."
>
> The Spirit of God says, "Beware, beware, the enemy roams about seeking whom he can devour and this sitting President is doing just that in this hour. He's full of lies and deceit and is very hateful; he spreads division and corruption with every mouthful. Beware when he says, 'Look over here, what the right hand is doing,' to divert your attention from what the left hand is doing, is his intention. This is a setup from this President and his minions, from the hate, the division, and Hillary Clinton. Why can

no one see this? For the signs are clear to see, that this President and his minions shall try for three. A sign will be, he will try and take the guns so the people can't rise up and stop him when he tries to run. He will not succeed, for this is the peoples' right, but make no mistake, it will be a fight."

The Spirit of God says, "My Army, My Army, rise up and take to the fight, and I will stop this that has already taken flight. For this is a war over America and not to be taken lightly. You will have to fight, but America will shine brightly. Take the fight to the enemy and you will be victorious for all to see, and America will be loved once again, even by some that used to be her enemies. My Army, continue to war, pray and fight with a shout, and I will remove this President that has become a louse! Then you will see the man I have chosen, Donald Trump, when he takes back MY WHITE HOUSE!"

People in high places who think their kingdom will not fall could take a lesson from the story of the writing on the wall found in the fifth chapter of Daniel.

The city outside was surrounded by military and was under threat of siege. However, the king obviously was not concerned, because he was inside his palace holding a feast, whereupon he became drunk and demanded that the vessels taken from the Jewish temple in Jerusalem be brought to him so that he, his princes, his wives, and even his concubines could drink wine from the sacred vessels. Using these items as they worshipped their false gods in a drunken indulgence was blasphemy the Lord could not tolerate. When a hand appeared and wrote on the wall, it was God sending a message to this king who was committing sacrilege. The king became terrified and wanted to know what the message meant, but even the king's wise men could not interpret the words, so Daniel was brought in. The king offered him material wealth in trade for explanation, which Daniel rejected. Daniel simply delivered the message:

And thou his son, O Belshazzar, hast not humbled thine heart, though thou knewest all this; But hast lifted up thyself against the Lord of heaven; and they have brought vessels of his house before thee, and thou, and thy lords, thy wives, and thy concubines, have drunk wine in them; and thou hast praised the gods of silver, and gold, of brass iron, wood, and stone, which see not, nor hear, nor know: and the God in whose hand thy breath is, and whose are all thy ways, hast thou not glorified: Then was the part of the hand sent from him; and this writing was written. And this is the writing that was written, Mene, Mene, Tekel, Upharsin. This is the interpretation of the thing: Mene; God hath numbered thy kingdom, and finished it. Tekel; Thou art weighed in the balances, and art found wanting. Peres; Thy kingdom is divided, and given to the Medes and Persians. Then commanded Belshazzar, and they clothed Daniel with scarlet, and put a chain of gold about his neck, and made a proclamation concerning him, that he should be the third ruler in the kingdom. In that night was Belshazzar the king of the Chaldeans slain.

DANIEL 5:22–30

Daniel was not motivated by material rewards, but instead told the king what God was saying to him for the mere sake of its being a message from the Divine. Daniel told the king that his kingdom would soon be divided. It happened straightaway. That very night, the king was slain in an invasion by an opposing army.

Those who are evil, who live as though there is no tomorrow, are living in a false security that they are in control of their world and that it will not change. They see the ill-gotten gains of the tangible world around them and presume that success is enduring. They are like the man in Luke 12:20, to whom God says, "Thou fool, this night thy soul shall be required of thee: then whose shall those things be, which thou hast provided?"

God is watching, and to those who have been given most, most will be required. Some of these people have had access to all the money and power one could ever wish for, and have used it for their own immoral gain. The wealth they enjoy is blood money. The blood of the innocents is on their hands, and God will hold them accountable.

Understand that blood literally cries out to God. This has been documented since the beginning of the earth.

> *And he said, What hast thou done? the voice of thy*
> *brother's blood crieth unto me from the ground.*
> GENESIS 4:10

Don't think for one moment that God doesn't hate the fact that the blood of innocents has been spilled out. The Bible is also very clear on this matter:

> *These six things doth the Lord hate:*
> *yea, seven are an abomination unto him:*
> *A proud look, a lying tongue,*
> *and hands that shed innocent blood,*
> *An heart that deviseth wicked imaginations,*
> *feet that be swift in running to mischief,*
> *A false witness that speaketh lies,*
> *and he that soweth discord among brethren.*
> PROVERBS 6:16–19

Does the description of this passage remind you of any people groups you know? Some of our authority figures in this country are guilty of any and all of these very acts. God hears the cries of all the innocent blood that has been shed. But remember, He does not exist in our understanding of time. He will operate within His own perfect timing. He is a God of action, and when He decides that the hour has come, this innocent blood will be avenged.

Will There Be Arrests?

As *Charisma News* has pointed out with the help of WikiLeaks: "We already have the FBI reopening its investigation into her private email server used while she was secretary of state. There are still thousands of the promised 50,000 emails yet to be released as part of the 'Podesta Emails' dossier, but Assange has assured the world this next round will offer 'enough evidence to see Hillary Clinton arrested.'"[95]

The anticipation of a possible arrest on this front has been just beneath the surface for quite some time now. As I stated before, some were convinced that if Clinton wasn't president, she'd be in prison. Will that happen? I believe so, and when it does, it will be a sign that the Jezebel spirit that has been over the United States has been locked up, with the key thrown away.

The Clinton Foundation right now has many forms of corruption that need to be investigated and prosecuted. Again, I believe this process will happen like dominoes. When big names start getting dropped and we see Hillary Clinton go down, I believe it will be the beginning of many investigations and arrest warrants that will create a many job openings in Washington.

Just within the Clinton Foundation alone, we have seen so much scandal that there is not enough space in this book to elaborate upon it all. Suffice it to say, this extremely corrupt machine has amassed immeasurable sums of criminal money, been entangled in multiple sexual scandals while in the public eye, abused privileged information and connections within state agencies, including Internal Revenue Service affiliations, participated in illegal campaign activities of all sorts, and has even managed to pass the buck on varieties of falsified or "missing" reports and documents.

Some of the scandals to which we will find the Clinton name attached right at the hub are the "Clinton U" scam, Filegate, WikiLeaks,

Emailgate, Chinagate, Whitewater, Travelgate, and Pardongate. These don't address other attacks, such as Benghazi, and the ever-growing list of the Clintons' friends who "committed suicide." Being a friend to the Clinton Foundation runs people the risk that they will either be tainted with blood money, end up in prison, or turn up dead. These people move in circles with high-end, shady world powers, and they keep tight associations with those who do not have America's best interest in mind.

But God has told me that time is up for those who are corrupt. He is coming to pass judgment on those who have ignored His voice and committed these atrocities.

Why the Supreme Court Must Be the Next to Change

God is beginning to make changes from the top down. In 2011, He told me that he had ordained a new type of presidential figure for this country by selecting Trump, but that was only the beginning. When people pray and begin to make a change from the top down, not only does the transformation have to happen with the role of the highest leader, but it is necessary to rearrange his surrounding advisors, peers, and supporting staff as well. There was a time when leaders had godly advisors.

This will happen again.

God is not finished making changes in this country. He plans to completely transform the justice system. As He told me the day I wrote this word above, "Time is up for those who are corrupt." He means it. He goes on to say in the second half of this work that the best days are ahead of us; He intends to clean house throughout our entire government.

To understand why this transformation is so important, we must comprehend the nature of the Supreme Court's role in our country. The court consists of nine justices, and as the name states, it carries an ultimate authority within our country:

The Supreme Court has a special role to play in the United States system of government. The Constitution gives it the power to check, if necessary, the actions of the President and Congress.

It can tell a President that his actions are not allowed by the Constitution. It can tell Congress that a law it passed violated the U.S. Constitution and is, therefore, no longer a law. It can also tell the government of a state that one of its laws breaks a rule in the Constitution.

The Supreme Court is the final judge in all cases involving laws of Congress, and the highest law of all—the Constitution.[96]

Because the president nominates the justice who will serve within this realm, the outcome of any election has a direct effect on what type of person will serve in the Supreme Court as positions become vacant. Our nation's most vital ruling force will hereby be indirectly decided by the election. This openly affects basically all vital legislation in our country.

Understand how absolutely critical the current state of our Supreme Court is. It is one of the final federal authorities in our country. It regulates essential elements of our legislation nationwide. A conservative, Bible-believing president who will nominate like-minded justices to serve in this role can tip the scale during these dynamic times of decision. Supreme Court justices serve for the duration of their own "good behavior," which can mean indefinitely. With that being said, it can be collectively assumed that a panel of justices who serve honorably and ethically could change the direction of this country and set us into a victorious cycle for many years to come.

Death of Scalia

The death of Justice Scalia was indeed a blow to conservative citizens throughout our country. It also left a key element, our national

Supreme Court, understaffed and vulnerable during a peak moment in our nation's history. As the election of 2016 raged on, it was suspended between two candidates that could not have been more opposite from one another. Simultaneously, the future position of this powerful, decisive entity, hung in the balance.

When Associate Justice Antonin Scalia passed away, it left the Supreme Court almost gridlocked on many vital decisions. We can see from the CNN Politics Online excerpt below the crucial nature of the decisions being made at the time of his death and the situation the Supreme Court was facing:

> They may be headed toward a 4-4 split in another case brought by religious non-profits to Obamacare's contraceptive mandate.
>
> At arguments, the eight justices seemed closely divided. Then, they released an unusual order asking for more briefs in the case—a clear indication that the justices are looking for a way to avoid a 4-4 split that could leave parts of the country living under different rules.
>
> The current term has no shortage of other high profile cases on issues such as abortion, affirmative action and immigration, and there may be more 4-4 opinions on the horizon highlighting the fact that the four liberal justices were nominated by Democratic presidents, while the four conservatives by Republicans.[97]

The change that is happening within the Supreme Court is only one of many ways that authority in very high places is divided down the middle at this time. A transition from the old charge to the new is underway, and as God has promised us that He is, and will continue to, clean house.

A prophetic word given to me on February 24, 2016 called "Do Not Fear, America" reads as follows:

The Spirit of God says, "Why do I sense fear in My people about the future of America? Have I not said that 'I have heard your cries and will heal your land?' Stand firm! Do not falter, put on the full armor of God! Rake the enemy over the coals, for the end time battle is on for my 1 billion souls!"

The Spirit of God says, "Do not fear that my servant Justice Scalia has been taken, for some are crying out, why have I forsaken. For I will show Myself strong to prove that the so-called wise are wrong. For some will say that this is a miracle, for I am just getting started, this is not even close to the pinnacle, for what I am going to do with My America. For do not My people have eyes to see and ears to hear the two signs I gave, when they carried My servant's body up the steps of the courthouse where to rest he was laid? Read the signs! Read the signs that were for all to see, and understand the words in this prophecy."

The Spirit of God says, "5, that's right, 5 Supreme Court Justices will be appointed by My new president, My anointed. I will choose 5 through My anointed to keep those alive. I will stack the court with those that I choose, to send a clear message to the enemy, that you lose! This is the miracle that I will perform, so that MY COURT will be reformed."

The Spirit of God says, "The cries, the cries that I have heard from the womb, have reached My eyes and ears like a sonic boom! The five I appoint and the reform that shall take place, the great I AM shall take on this case! For it is My will and My way for all those that have prayed, that MY COURT SHALL OVERTURN ROE VS WADE!"

The Spirit of God says, "America, get ready, for I AM choosing from the top of the cream, for I AM putting together America's dream team, from the president and his administration, to judges and congress to ease America's frustrations!"

The Spirit of God says, "Rise up, My Army, and get in

the fight, for this is the generation that's taking flight. This is the generation of warriors that those of old wanted to see, and the enemy will have no choice but to flee. Rise up! Stomp the enemy's head with bliss; send the enemy back to Hell and into the abyss. This is the generation of warriors that all of Hell has feared to face and see, but I AM and all of Heaven is cheering you on with glee!

"Your Supreme Commander, God"

This prophecy begins with a reminder of God promises: *if my people...* There it is again! God is continuously faithful and reminds us that we need only repent and turn to Him for healing of our lives, our families, our churches, and in this case, our land.

Roe v. Wade

We are in the process of seeing these prophecies unfold right before our eyes at this very moment. Some elements of this word were literally hanging in the balance, suspended, while the election of 2016 was underway. Since the president nominates individuals who will serve in the Supreme Court, the choice of candidates between Clinton and Trump was a matter of utmost difference for our Supreme Court. The elected candidate would set the tone for the future of many pertinent legal issues facing our country. *Roe v. Wade* is only one legal matter that loomed eminently for the future of America. See below what Dan Mangan of *CNBC News* says of the candidates' responses to just this one issue:

"I am pro-life," Trump said during Wednesday night's presidential debate when asked whether he wanted that decision, *Roe v. Wade*, reversed by the Supreme Court.

Trump said that if the ruling were to be reversed, laws on the legality or illegality of abortion would "go back to the individual states" to decide, which was the case prior to *Roe v. Wade*.

But when moderator Chris Wallace pressed him on whether he wanted the ruling overturned, Trump said, "That will happen, automatically in my opinion," because he would get to nominate potentially several justices to the court.

In response, Hillary Clinton said, "I strongly support *Roe v. Wade*."

"I will defend *Roe v. Wade*, I will defend a woman's right to make her own decision," Clinton said.[98]

You can see by just this one interaction how the outcome of the 2016 election was essential to the position of the Supreme Court on imperative issues. This is where we come in. As Christians, it is our job to take a stand and elect and pray for the right individuals. We simply *must* stop saying that the Church and/or God doesn't belong in politics, because if we take a backseat on these issues, we are leaving the lost to their own devices, and we are leaving believers to live in a world legislated by those without biblical conviction (and everything that implies for us on a moral level daily; more on this in the upcoming chapters).

The "if my people" element to this situation could have played out like this: A victory for Clinton would have meant that fruition of the *Roe v. Wade* prophecy above would have been postponed for a good while, in keeping with the principles that I explained in a previous chapter wherein I discussed God's relationship between time and man's actions. We would have been placing someone in the position of essential influence and authority who would have done her best to obstruct God's will, delaying America's blessing. On the importance of the selection of individuals for service within the Supreme Court, Americans United for Life's Acting President Clarke Forsythe said:

When *Roe v. Wade* was arbitrarily decided by the Supreme Court, without medical evidence or a trial court record of thorough debate, abortion on demand was created out of thin air, based on judicial preferences. It was a sweeping act of judicial overreach and a premier example of what legislating from the bench looks like. A judiciary committed to interpreting—not creating law—is key for respecting the voice of the people through their elected officials.[99]

Consider Jeremiah 19:5–6:

> *They have built also the high places of Baal,*
> *to burn their sons with fire for burnt offerings unto Baal,*
> *which I commanded not, nor spake it, neither came it into my*
> *mind: Therefore, behold, the days come, saith the LORD,*
> *that this place shall no more be called Tophet, nor*
> *The valley of the son of Hinnom, but The valley of slaughter.*

These people literally sacrificed their children to Ba'al, in hopes of avoiding crisis or disaster, and of increasing their wealth and prosperity. Sound like any modern society you know of?

Trump Will Replace Five

I had originally prophesied that three judges would be caught in a scandal and subsequently they would be dismissed of their responsibilities or step down: "The Spirit of God says, "The Supreme Court shall lose three, and My President shall pick new ones directly from MY TREE!"

Later, God told me that, in addition to this, one would pass away (and it would not be who we think) and one would retire. This means that Trump will replace a total of five justices while he is in office.

Are you starting to grasp just how essential this situation is for the future of our country? There are nine positions in the Supreme Court, and Trump will be replacing five! Because God's anointed will be nominating these individuals, He *really is* going to reform the judicial system! This will be met with resistance, and we Christians have to pray our country through this upcoming time of turbulence and not become discouraged by the friction as these changes occur. This is because of how vital the role of the Supreme Court is. Remember, forces of evil do not give up their seat without a fight!

They still wait for their opportunity to see the tides turn again to their favor, as we can see by the following quote. Although this was written before the election of 2016 ended, it reflects the hopeful attitude of those who intently await the opportunity to see the Supreme Court filled with liberals again. Pro-choicers like Ian Millhiser are waiting anxiously to see what direction the Supreme Court, and hence our country, will move:

> The choice whether to hold the case over could also matter for an entirely different reason. If President Obama (or a similarly minded president) manages to fill Justice Scalia's seat, one of the first matters taken up by the Court's new liberal majority would be a major abortion case. That would not only give them the opportunity to strike down HB2, it would also give them the chance to expand a right to choose that has been gradually chipped away after decades of conservative decisions. The vague "undue burden" standard that now controls abortion cases was pushed by abortion opponents including the Reagan Justice Department and AUL [American's United for Life] before it was ultimately adopted by the Supreme Court. A more liberal Court could scrap this standard altogether or, at the very least, clarify it in a way that does not permit anti-abortion judges to take advantage of its vagueness...

Yet that outcome depends entirely on who gets to fill Justice Scalia's seat. If the next justice is more like Scalia, Whole Woman's Health could still become AUL's greatest triumph.

[Millhiser later goes on to say:] Except that opponents of abortion no longer have the fifth vote they need to gut Roe. Justice Antonin Scalia's death means that Roe shall live at least another year. Whether it survives past next year, however, could very well be decided by whoever gets to fill Scalia's seat.[100]

Understand that this potentially will be a very tumultuous time for our country. The enemy will not let go without a fight. In fact, right now he has dug in his claws with extreme determination. Powers of darkness feed on the blood of the innocent, and the laws that enable that blood to flow freely in this land are regulated by the Supreme Court. This places the court at dead center of every spiritual stronghold that fights to keep this nation captive.

This is, again, where you and I come in. This is where we hold the ground we have taken. We absolutely must pray our new president through the times ahead and see the next phases of the battle to completion. We won the election, but Trump has many battles ahead of him that we must call God's presence down upon each and every day. Because the 2016 election turned out as it did, we can be confident that Trump will search for a like-minded person to serve in this capacity. However, a victory for Clinton would have been a disaster for this and many other pertinent legal and spiritual matters facing this country. As I have repeatedly stated, God loves America and has chosen her. But recall how I discussed in the previous chapter that God hates the shedding of innocent blood. America must stay on track with the over-turning of a new leaf, because we must stop this practice of abortion. God will no longer tolerate it. If we refuse to obey, we could interrupt our own ability to accept the blessing He has for us, just as we did in 2012, when He looked at us and found us not yet ready to receive.

UPDATE: The Supreme Court

A while after prophesying that Trump would replace three officials within the Supreme Court, the Lord spoke to Mark Taylor regarding an additional two that He wanted removed. Upon sharing this bold statement, Mark caught the attention of many naysayers, but the news was met with anticipatory speculation as those within the Obama administration began clamoring to fill the empty seat left behind by Antonin Scalia in February of 2016. Nominating Merrick Garland for the position, President Obama's efforts were subsequently barricaded by Senate Majority Leader Mitch McConnell, who declared that the next President Elect—who, at that time, was yet to be determined—should be the one who chooses a nominee to fill the seat.[101]

In June of 2018, Justice Anthony M. Kennedy announced his retirement from the Supreme Court, realizing the second open seat that Trump would reassign.[102]

In 2016, when Mark wrote the prophecy entitled *Do Not Fear, America*, there were specific items that he said God had ordained for the U.S. Supreme Court. Beyond the fact that five new justices would be appointed by Donald Trump, we were told that the president's appointments would consist of individuals who would honor God's righteousness, reforming the Supreme Court from the inside out, thus impacting our entire nation's justice system. Furthermore, Mark's prophetic word states that God, Himself, would overhaul the U.S. Judicial System from the top-down, assembling the "dream team, from the President and his administration, to judges and congress to ease America's frustrations!"

President Trump has been crucial to the modifications taking place within our judicial system at present, and the court system in our country is certainly seeing a turnover of officials. The numeric shift to more conservative seat-holders all throughout the justice system has already summed to quite a list. As of now, Trump has appointed 29 conservative judges into federal circuit courts.[103] In addition, he has appointed two new Supreme Court justices: Neil Gorsuch and Brett Kavanaugh. As newcomers contribute to a conservative slant, speculation holds that other Supreme Court justices of retirement age will cling to their positions in order to keep liberal sway. However, Mark reminds us that God has decreed three more openings during the time of Donald Trump's administration.[104]

How will these seats become available? Mark answers by explaining that the details may never be announced in the media. At the source of the trouble will be some sort of scandal, and those who discontinue service will either step down willingly or will be asked to do so. Whether the scandal will be exposed openly or handled quietly Mark cannot say. He likewise acknowledges that the issue could be related to *Roe vs. Wade* or something different altogether, and furthermore does not assert that these openings will *necessarily* happen during Trump's first term as president. However, Mark maintains that regardless of whether the details emerge in the news or these justices disengage their office quietly, we can expect to see three more vacancies within the Supreme Court under Donald Trump.

Mark's prophetic word also relays the message from God that the cries of the aborted unborn have risen to His ears, and that He will soon rectify this by seeing the Supreme Court overturn *Roe vs. Wade*. Promises to do precisely that were made by Trump during his presidential campaign; however, many individuals speculated that he would have trouble persuading the Supreme Court to take such action. A surprising turn of events could be coming, according to those who observe Kennedy's resignation as the absence of a "swing vote" that may have impeded the potential reversal. Jim Carlin, Iowan Republican state senator, was quoted: "With (Kennedy) as the swing vote, I don't know that we would have had the capital on the Supreme Court to reverse *Roe v. Wade*... If we were to get another conservative justice to the bench at the Supreme Court, I think our chances are much, much higher."[105]

Perhaps this was the real reason behind the opposition to instating

Judge Brett Kavanaugh into the Supreme Court. The man had established himself as one who supports the "separation of powers" doctrine of the U.S. Constitution, as believing in federal agency accountability and reasonable limitation, a supporter of spiritual liberty and religious employers' rights, and freedom of speech.[106]

Mark reminds the Body of Christ to be in prayer over the issue of the coming scandal pertaining to three Justices. He recalls our attention to the tumult that the American populace has endured during each of these two previous, single vacancies within the Supreme Court, explaining that if *one* opening can create such an upheaval, then the impending discord resulting from *three* resignations at or near the same time could mean a period of vast friction within our society. Beginning now to immerse the matter in prayer can be the difference in the future of our country's entire Judicial System.

Mark's prophetic word, written in February of 2016, ends with an endorsement for the Body of Christ to stay in the fight. And as Mark has told us, this is done by praying, taking a stand and speaking out, and continuing to be participants within the political realm. This is scriptural, as even the Word reminds us: "For we wrestle not against flesh and blood, but against principalities, against powers, against the rulers of the darkness of this world, against spiritual wickedness in high places" Ephesians 6:12.

———

There Is Evil in the Courtroom

I have a dear, close friend who works for the federal government, within the court system. This person works for a very prestigious judge who has been on the bench for several decades, and who is a very conservative Christian. The judge recently had an event celebrating an employment anniversary, and I was invited to attend via this same contact. The event was large, with nearly twenty other judges in attendance. Throughout the evening, something kept stirring in my spirit. It was very ominous and distinct. I kept feeling a sensation on my head, similar to some strange type of electricity. Throughout the evening, a bizarre awareness of a strange, looming presence that I could not see kept returning. I kept asking God, "Lord, what is this? What is happening?"

I remember noticing at the time that the individual whom the event was honoring had a letter, thanking him for his many years of service. I listened as it was read aloud. I wondered if the people surrounding me had any clue what I had prophesied regarding their system. I recalled the words I had foretold, and found myself curious about whether I was in the presence of any of the people I had written about. I wondered if they knew who I was, what I had predicted, or how it would make them feel to know that I had foretold the downfall of some of their comrades.

All of a sudden I realized that the sensations I had been having were of a cautionary nature. I realized that I was on spiritually dangerous ground. I had been speaking out against the powers of evil that have strongholds in high places, yet I had ventured right into their territory!

I left as soon afterward as I could politely do so, and returned home. That night I had by far the most sinister visitation I have ever had. This was unlike any I had experienced before. A malicious entity appeared in my room. It's hard to even describe. Unlike the others previously, this time, I had no waves—no warning that this one was coming. I abruptly found myself accompanied in bed by a very dark presence that just appeared from behind. It lay behind me on the bed, where I was unable to turn to see it, and placed its hand over my mouth so that I could not speak. I could not call for help.

It was demonic. And very powerful.

I knew immediately that it was trying to intimidate me, attempting to keep me from speaking or prophesying. I struggled, trying to get words out, but I was unable to utter a sound. But without doubt I understood *very* clearly its message to me: "Do not come near the court, and do not speak out against the evil within it again."

By this time, I had become accustomed to enduring visitations that I would have, and my wife, Mari Jo, was used to seeing me go through this experience as well. She understands not to wake me up if she sees that I am showing signs of unrest, because if I am receiving a message or going through some kind of required interaction within the spirit realm, it is necessary for me to find my own way through it. She will often pray for me and watch over me until the event is finished, but she does not usually intervene.

On this particular night, however, she later told me that something had been different about this instance. Instead of my breathing holding the irregular pattern she has come to expect during these happenings, this time, I was screaming—but I wasn't aware of the cries I was outwardly, physically giving. From my perspective in the visitation with this evil behind me, I was only aware that I was being silenced. It wasn't until my wife told me that I found out I had been shouting for help.

Because Mari Jo normally allows me to press through the experience uninterrupted while she prays for me, she allowed this to continue for what she told me was several seconds. To me, it felt like a much longer period of time. After this, she decided she had "seen enough," and she began to shake me, calling my name and doing all she could to wake me up. When I didn't respond, she placed her hands on either side of my face, shaking my head, and after what she remembers to be about fifteen seconds, I finally came to. I sat on the bed for quite some time, attempting to regain my composure. I had never encountered an entity like that before. I'm not sure exactly what rank within the powers of darkness that entity held, but it was much more powerful than those that had visited me in my earlier experiences.

This experience also affected Mari Jo, who has never been one to have visitations such as these until recently, when I began to prophecy about the court system. Before this, I had been the sole target of these disturbances. But the night when the entities became more menacing, they also broadened their target range. They began to harass Mari Jo as well.

One night shortly thereafter, as Mari Jo was asleep, she began breathing heavily, and tossing somewhat as though she were having a nightmare. I placed my hand on her shoulder and shook her until she woke up. My wife doesn't have many dreams, so when she has one she knows is of importance, I listen to her.

This is the dream that she told me she had: She was in the courtroom addressing a group of people, explaining that the actual courtroom wasn't necessarily an evil in itself, but that there was certainly evil *within* it. If they were to pray *against* the evil, she said, they would be safe from it. Next, she began to teach the people how to pray with authority over the evil to cast it out, and she was immediately attacked by multiple wicked spirits. It was as she began to struggle against them, hopelessly outnumbered, that I woke her up.

Earlier that same day, I had met my friend who works within the court system for lunch. All I had done was set foot on the property of the courthouse, and that same night Mari Jo had this attack. And every time I have so much as stepped on the property since the day of the anniversary event, something ominous has happened. Something malevolent is attached to our court system, and it does not want those who pray or speak out against it to even set foot on that territory.

As the people Mari Jo and I are associated with begin to pray with us in agreement against the forces of evil in the judicial system, many of them are increasingly being subjected to attacks as well. Some of the occurrences are so out of the blue and inexplicable that they can only be described as simply unreal. I'm surrounded by those who have stood with me in prayer, and who are now suffering every kind of onslaught you can think of: physical illness, financial hardship, previously successful businesses unexpectedly failing, spouses abruptly leaving, and many other events that have begun barraging these people as they have banded together in prayer.

Things Are Heating Up

There have been other instances when an inexplicable event happened while I have been writing a prophetic word. One example had taken place on July 14, 2016, not terribly long before Mari Jo had her awful dream. Keeping up with the preliminary activities of the GOP convention, I was at home alone, sitting at the breakfast bar in my kitchen writing a prophetic word when I was abruptly interrupted by a strange *thud*. My mind was jolted out of what I was doing by the suddenness of the noise on an otherwise tranquil day.

I looked around for a moment and continued to write.

There it was again.

Thud.

Only this time it didn't happen once; there were several *thuds*. I moved my pencil back toward the paper with intention of attempting to write again, until the sound occurred a third time. Sporadic fits of thudding sounds were now a constant part of the background noise in the room. It was terribly distracting. I stood up and looked around, trying to locate the source of the sound. As I walked across the room, I spotted some motion from the corner of my eye near the window. As I turned to investigate, I realized that I had been hearing the sounds of two birds, each about the size of a blue jay, and with a nondescript, grayish hue, fighting each other right outside my window. As they clashed with each other, they repeatedly collided with the window.

I shook my head lightly, dismissing the occurrence as a fluke of regular wildlife behavior. I live in the country, and it's not abnormal for a bird to occasionally hit the window. I picked up my pad and pencil from the breakfast bar and made way for the office located on the other side of the house, where I could shut the door and drown out the distracting sound of the two combatant birds.

I sat down at my desk and continued to write. A moment later, I was interrupted by yet another loud *thud*. After a second or two, the sound became rhythmic again, a constant beat of the fighting birds hitting against the window of my office. At that point, I thought it was pretty strange. For a bird to collide with a window once is not unusual, but for two birds, fighting each other within moments, to find their way completely around the house and collide repeatedly with the window in the room I had moved to, was just uncanny.

Strange coincidence…

I again picked up my pad and pencil and walked back to the breakfast bar, only to have this event repeat, again. I tried other rooms, and the happening continued. They persisted to follow me wherever I went. Then, as I approached the window near the breakfast bar again, I saw small speckles of blood on the glass, as though the birds had fought until they were bleeding and continued to pound each other's bodies against my house. For both to stay engaged in the fight at that point was out of character for birds of this size, as far as I knew.

As I approached the glass for a closer look at this, I noticed something odd about my truck parked right outside. The blood spatter that was now sprinkled on the window of my house was only a small comparison to the amount of blood splattered all over my truck's windshield.

To be clear, there were not gallons of blood as though a human being had bled out all over the place, but there were flecks of red blood, like raindrops, all over my truck's windshield in one straight line across the bottom seven inches. Although not a complete and total bloodbath, for small birds, it was a lot of blood. I have seen an incredible amount of blood in my time as a fireman, and I had never seen anything like that. Even the splatter pattern was too precise and linear to represent a normal, animalistic battle. And despite the fight that I had witnessed, there didn't appear to be a lost feather anywhere. Bird defecation was also spread all over the vehicle. A single dropping or two of bird excretion was unusual for this time of year and in that parking location, but the sheer volume of it was like nothing I had ever witnessed. The whole thing was very reminiscent of a scene that might have been written into Alfred Hitchcock's *The Birds*.

I suspected that either God was going to reveal something important to me, or the enemy was trying to obstruct me from writing. Deciding to prevent the latter, I called a friend of mine at the time and asked her to pray with me. She agreed to pray immediately and we hung up the phone. Thirty minutes later, she called me back.

She indicated to me that the Lord was telling her that there would be an attack, that blood would be spilled, and that a vehicle would be involved. We agreed to pray and intercede regarding the impending event. We weren't sure what we were even praying for at that point, we only knew that God would intervene and provide His peace and healing in a dynamic way.

Not four hours later, a cargo vehicle killed more than eighty people by driving into crowds who were celebrating Bastille Day in Nice, France. We didn't know any of the individuals that day personally, but we had been in intercession for them all afternoon. The Lord had showed me by the blood all over my truck that an attack was coming and that I should be in prayer for those who would be affected. He did not tell me where the attack would be or give me a prophetic word regarding the event on this occasion. This time the only intervention He called me to was prayer.

Often, when a bird collides with a window, the oils and dirt within its feathers leave smudges—a tell-tale sign of where it struck. On this occasion, however, there were no such marks. Only the blood splash remained. Afterward, when I told this story, I was asked many questions. Why didn't God give me a prophetic word so that I could warn people and save lives? Why didn't the birds leave smudges on the windows? Did I believe the birds were real, physical entities or something supernatural? Why *birds*, and not other creatures, like squirrels or rabbits?

I will answer these questions to the best of my ability: I do not know why sometimes God tells me what is coming and other times He does not. I do not know why the birds did not leave smudges; I would not rule out anything where God is concerned. He may have chosen to use "real" birds, or they could have existed only in the spirit realm. They *appeared* real to my physical eyes, but anything is possible with God, and He can use any means He chooses to get the attention of His people to prophesy, pray, or otherwise take action toward what He is instructing. We are all part of His plan and need to be in tune with His voice.

One thing I know for sure: The blood and excrement left behind were certainly real, whether the birds were or not, because I pulled out my cell phone and took pictures of the truck and window after the event. Others who have seen these photos have agreed that the blood patterns are highly irregular. If a person had wanted to simulate this on his or her own—say, for attention or some other showy purpose—he or she would have likely made it look like a brawl between two wild animals had taken place with sporadic droplets everywhere. I couldn't have staged this, and I couldn't have known hours beforehand that a cargo truck was going to kill people at a gathering in France later that day, *unless* the Lord was giving me that information—in which case, the Lord's involvement cancels out a "staged" phenomenon. The whole ordeal was unbelievable.

But just as I had seen strange occurrences as a direct result of my involvement with the prophetic word, Mari Jo was now being pulled into this world. Some entity out there didn't want the people of God praying for the Lord's will in the judicial system, and things were getting heated. Her nightmare of the courtroom was proof enough of that for me.

Do Not Be Afraid!

God has told me that He is choosing His dream team to run this country. Transition is always hard and change is often met with resistance, but God has promised us He will clean house! I am a firm believer that the next generation of our country's leaders will come forth from God's remnant. Imagine what this country will be like when the Army of God prevails and the leadership is godly.

God will lead the transformation within the judicial system of this country. He will bring in His chosen, just as He did with Trump, and they will begin to legislate according to righteous standards. The government will have a place for godly advisors again, and our country will thrive.

God has chosen our president. He will lead our president in choosing his supporting staff and leaders, especially within the judicial system. God has promised us that He will clean house in our government and we can count on Him to follow through.

The laws of this land have to change in order for us to return to the days of our prosperity. It is time for the laws of our land to align with biblical morals again. We need to invite God back into our legal system, back into our courtroom, and evict the evil that currently resides there.

God has ordained that, once again, there *will* be order in the court.

chapter eight

A Glorious Church, Without Spot or Wrinkle

The Church is in trouble. The Church has been duped. The Church has unwittingly signed a deal with Ba'al.

Do I have your attention yet?

Many people these days are saying that America is under judgment. Let me be very clear: *America* is not. The *systems* are, and specifically, it's the *Church* that's under judgment. Judgment starts in the house of the Lord.

In the first paragraph of the word I wrote called "Let My People Go" in July of 2016, I wrote: "The Spirit of God says, 'When Donald Trump is elected, a sign will be given. The earth shall quake because of who I have selected.'"

On November 14, 2016, just six days after Trump was elected, there was a major earthquake in the city of Christchurch, New Zealand (South Island, Canterbury Region). I knew that this was the earthquake that God was referring to because He told me that the quake would serve as a sign that He was going to shake up His church. The area struck by the seismic activity was also dealing with a series of tsunami waves at the time. This was God's way of saying that the judgment was on Christ's Church and that the aftermath was going to appear in waves.

We've already seen the first wave in the form of a massive exodus from the Church because so many people have had enough of the "organized establishment" that the Church has become. Congregations are losing numbers left and right. Whether it's spiritual, financial, moral, or whatever the individual case may be, there is just far too much corruption to hold its audience anymore.

Why is the Body of Christ under judgment, and exactly *how is most of it under contract with Ba'al today?* God showed me in April of 2016 when I wrote the following word, "Purging the Temple":

The Spirit of God says, "The 501(c)(3), the 501(c)(3), those that are eating of it are not eating from My tree! For when I told Adam and Eve, 'Do not eat from the Tree of the Knowledge of Good and Evil, for you shall surely see,' so it is with those that eat from the 501(c)(3). For this demonic document that you have signed has now made you spiritually deaf, mute, and blind. Woe to those who continue to use this demonic system, for you will be exposed and purged from this evil cistern."

This Spirit of God says, "Can you not see that you are taking a bribe? They will say it's all about the money, and for that you shall by kicked from My tribe! Taking a bite from that apple has taken you from a spiritual Body to a brick-and-mortar, and has placed you under the New World Order. For how can you be a part of My spiritual Body when you have cut off My head? For those that don't turn will surely fall as dead. Tear up the contract, repent, divorce Ba'al, and re-marry Me, and I will remove the spiritual blindness so you can once again see. Come out of this! Come out of this before it's too late, for My judgments are on those systems that I hate. Come out now for I will no longer tolerate!"

The Johnson Amendment

In order to explain further why the 501(c)(3) is so dangerous to the Church, allow me to bring you up to speed on some pertinent history.

In 1954, churches were added to the 501(c)(3) section of the federal tax code. Senator Lyndon Johnson was the man mainly responsible for this action, which is why it's called the "Johnson Amendment." Under this new law, churches were now able to attain the tax-free status, and were no longer required to pay taxes.

Wait a minute...

Churches *were already tax exempt.* So, what was the motive behind this action? Well, it's certainly a debated point. Let's take a look at it a little more closely.

Under the policy as it pertains to the 501(c)(3), a tax-exempt religious organization cannot speak out on the essential issues facing our current society. Some would argue that what it *actually states* is that the individual church under contract is prohibited from backing a *specific political candidate.* While this is true, a little digging into the policy reveals a lot of fine print that actually restricts the church much further, keeping it from saying or doing much of anything within political realms (and so, *so* much more). See the IRS definition below:

The Restriction of Political Campaign Intervention by Section 501(c)(3) Tax-Exempt Organizations

Under the Internal Revenue Code, all section 501(c)(3) organizations are absolutely prohibited from directly or indirectly participating in, or intervening in, any political campaign on behalf of (or in opposition to) any candidate for elective public office. Contributions to political campaign funds or public statements of position (verbal or written) made on behalf of the organization in favor of or in opposition to any candidate for public office clearly violate the prohibition against political campaign activity. Violating this prohibition may result in denial or revocation of tax-exempt status and the imposition of certain excise taxes.

Certain activities or expenditures may not be prohibited depending on the facts and circumstances. For example, certain voter education activities (including presenting public forums and publishing voter education guides) conducted in a non-partisan manner do not constitute prohibited political campaign activity. In addition, other activities intended to encourage people to participate in the electoral process, such as voter registration and get-out-the-vote drives, would not be prohibited political campaign activity if conducted in a non-partisan manner.

On the other hand, voter education or registration activities with evidence of bias that (a) would favor one candidate over another; (b) oppose a candidate in some manner; or (c) have the effect of favoring a candidate or group of candidates, will constitute prohibited participation or intervention.[107]

Seems clear-cut enough so far, right? Pretty straightforward. The church participating in the 501(c)(3) code is not allowed to be as bold as to back an actual candidate specifically. Fair enough. But let's take a closer look at the *actual exemption requirements* taken directly from the IRS' website:

Exemption Requirements—501(c)(3) Organizations

To be tax-exempt under section 501(c)(3) of the Internal Revenue Code, an organization must be organized and operated exclusively for exempt purposes set forth in section 501(c)(3), and none of its earnings may inure to any private shareholder or individual. In addition, it may not be an *action organization,* i.e., it may not attempt to influence legislation as a substantial part of its activities and it may not participate in any campaign activity for or against political candidates.

Organizations described in section 501(c)(3) are commonly referred to as charitable organizations. Organizations described in section 501(c)(3), other than testing for public safety organizations, are eligible to receive tax-deductible contributions in accordance with Code section 170.

The organization must not be organized or operated for the benefit of private interests, and no part of a section 501(c)(3) organization's net earnings may inure to the benefit of any private shareholder or individual. If the organization engages in an excess benefit transaction with a person having substantial influence over the organization, an excise tax may be imposed on the person and any organization managers agreeing to the transaction.

Section 501(c)(3) organizations are restricted in how much political and legislative (lobbying) activities they may conduct. For a detailed discussion, see Political and Lobbying. For more information about lobbying activities by charities, see the article Lobbying Issues; for more information about political activities of charities, see the FY-2002 CPE topic Election Year Issues.[108]

Let's back up for a second here. Reread that if you need to. First of all, the church is not allowed to be an *action organization*...

Not allowed to be an action organization?!

Then *why in the world* are we even here? It goes on to explain that it may not attempt to influence legislation as a substantial part of its activities, and that it cannot back specific candidates. It is limited in its legislative and lobbying activities. Still not sure where this is going? Let's read farther into how the IRS specifically defines 501(c)(3) Legislative Activity and Lobbying:

Lobbying

In general, no organization may qualify for section 501(c)(3) status if a substantial part of its activities is attempting to influence legislation (commonly known as lobbying). A 501(c)(3) organization may engage in some lobbying, but too much lobbying activity risks loss of tax-exempt status.

Legislation includes action by Congress, any state legislature, any local council, or similar governing body, with respect to acts, bills, resolutions, or similar items (such as legislative confirmation of appointive office), or by the public in referendum, ballot initiative, constitutional amendment, or similar procedure. It does not include actions by executive, judicial, or administrative bodies.

An organization will be regarded as attempting to influence legislation if it contacts, or urges the public to contact, members or employees of a legislative body for the purpose of proposing, supporting, or opposing legislation, or if the organization advocates the adoption or rejection of legislation.

Organizations may, however, involve themselves in issues of public policy without the activity being considered as lobbying. For example, organizations may conduct educational meetings, prepare and distribute educational materials, or otherwise consider public policy issues in an educational manner without jeopardizing their tax-exempt status.[109]

First of all, legislative action is defined as "action by Congress, any state legislature, any local council, or similar governing body, with respect to acts, bills, resolutions, or similar items (such as legislative confirmation of appointive office), or by the public in referendum, ballot initiative, constitutional amendment, or similar procedure." That pretty much covers anything regarding our government system as a whole, does it not? And I'm not trying to nitpick here, but the policy is completely subjective. Just how much lobbying is "some lobbying?" How is a church to know just how much lobbying is permissible, and when it has crossed the line?

Also, let's take a closer look at that middle section again: "An organization will be regarded as attempting to influence legislation if it contacts, or urges the public to contact, members or employees of a legislative body for the purpose of proposing, supporting, or opposing legislation, or if the organization advocates the adoption or rejection of legislation." This not only covers any action that the government might take, but also states that the church is out of line if it encourages its members to exercise *their rights as citizens* by suggesting that they contact their operating political representatives and authorities in order to be heard. Is this not the peaceable, constitutional way of letting our government know where we—the voters—stand on specific issues?

Then, in the last paragraph, they throw back into the mix just enough gray area to leave people feeling like maybe they still have a few rights. We are allowed to *educate*. We can hand out materials. Be careful! Don't try to impact or influence "with respect to acts, bills, resolutions, or similar items...or by the public in referendum, ballot initiative, constitutional amendment, or similar procedure, or advocate the adoption or rejection of legislation."

So what does it mean? It means the church is to *be silent*. We are allowed "some lobbying," which, I suppose, becomes restricted once our voices become annoying or begin to get in the way of the wrong party's agenda. But the nutshell?

Shhhh...

Don't speak out, or we could lose our tax-exempt status! (You know, that one we already had?!)

Think about the moral issues facing our modern-day Church. When a single woman at the end of her rope comes to our church's ladies group asking about abortion options, should we merely "educate" her without mentioning biblical conviction on the topic? A teenage boy facing peer pressure about drugs deserves more than cold, clinical "educational" feedback from a youth pastor he's confiding in regarding the physiological effects substance abuse has on the human body. That middle-aged man facing crisis about his sexual identity who wanders in to his local church for direction deserves more than an "educational" response from the prayer team who met him at the altar with facts about the disease risks of engaging in same-sex relations.

If these people wanted an "education," they would have looked up a public service announcement or gone to a governmentally subsidized clinic. They are in church because they want to know: "What does *God* think about this decision I'm facing? What is right? What is wrong? How will this decision affect me *morally* for the rest of my life?" It's about the *moral* code. Since Adam and Eve, it's been about morality, not public education seminars delivered with proverbial layers of duct tape over our mouths, lest we achieve more than "some" warning until we annoy someone in the government. Are we—the Body of Christ—going to be the Church or not?

No. As long as we belong under the oppression of the 501(c)(3)... we are not. We, the Church, have been silenced, all for those thirty pieces of silver.

Without the 501(c)(3)

Ironically, at the end of the day, none of this is even necessary. The 501(c)(3) isn't even required! Churches are already tax exempt, and *always have been in this country*. If they take away our 501(c)(3), where are we? Well, I'll tell you: back at the NON-501(c)(3), tax-exempt status we had *before 1954*. Remember the one? The one where we were both tax-exempt—*and*—allowed to speak out?

Let's see what the IRS itself has to say on this:

Automatic Exemption for Churches

Churches that meet the requirements of IRC Section 501(c)(3) are automatically considered tax exempt and are not required to apply for and obtain recognition of tax-exempt status from the IRS. Although there is no requirement to do so, many churches seek recognition of tax-exempt status from the IRS because this recognition assures church leaders, members and contributors that the church is recognized as exempt and qualifies for related tax benefits. For example, contributors to a church that has been recognized as tax exempt would know that their contributions generally are tax-deductible.[110]

So why adhere to it? Honestly, most often, it's out of ignorance. Many church leaders don't even realize they have the option. Numerous accountants and CPAs routinely recommend 501(c)(3) for a variety of reasons, and as churches are starting up or renewing paperwork, they innocently follow these instructions, not realizing that they are unwittingly inviting jurisdiction to which they were not previously subject. See how Peter Kershaw and Steve Nestor describe it below:

> Not only is it completely unnecessary for any church to seek 501(c)(3) status, to do so becomes a grant of jurisdiction to the IRS by any church that obtains that State favor. In the words of Steve Nestor, IRS Sr. Revenue Officer (ret.):
>
>> I am not the only IRS employee who's wondered why churches go to the government and seek permission to be exempted from a tax they didn't owe to begin with, and to seek a tax deductible status that they've always had anyway. Many of us have marveled at how church leaders want to be regulated and controlled by an agency of government that most Americans have prayed would

just get out of their lives. Churches are in an amazingly unique position, but they don't seem to know or appreciate the implications of what it would mean to be free of government control.[111]

Under Contract with Ba'al

Many people are unaware that Washington, DC, is filled with monuments to Ba'al. The Washington Monument itself is a symbol of honor to Ba'al, as are the shape and locations of the domes and many other features of the nation's capital, which would require their own book to elaborate upon (many of which have been written by the score already; give a quick Google search on the topic a try...). Understand this: Our nation's capital is basically an altar to Ba'al. Thus, it is not unreasonable to claim that placing our churches under the unnecessary jurisdiction of this entity in exchange for a monetary status, we are essentially placing it under contract with Ba'al.

By submitting to this entity, subjecting ourselves to its authority and allowing it to *buy our silence*, we basically place ourselves in agreement with its laws. This makes the Church guilty of the sins committed within the parameters of its laws. In the spirit realm, we are turning a blind eye.

> *And if a soul sin, and hear the voice of swearing,*
> *and is a witness, whether he hath seen or known of it;*
> *if he do not utter it, then he shall bear his iniquity.*
> LEVITICUS 5:1

I've said this before, and it bears repeating: The Church is to be the moral compass for its country. As the Church, we are called to be notably different than those around us.

They are not of the world,
even as I am not of the world.
JOHN 17:16

We are here on earth, but are supposed to be ambassadors for a higher Kingdom. We were never meant to be silently standing by, watching atrocities occur while our own voices are powerless.

But ye are a chosen generation, a royal priesthood, an holy nation,
a peculiar people; that ye should shew forth the praises of him who
hath called you out of darkness into his marvellous light.
1 PETER 2:9

All we need to do for any further confirmation of where we as the Church have placed ourselves is to take a look at the list of who our fiscally neighboring corporations are under the 501(c)(3). See this excerpt from an article by *Creation Liberty Evangelism Online* (the brackets surrounding the websites appeared in the original source; all other brackets were added for clarification):

Amazingly, some Christians will *still* question if being a part of the 501(c)(3) church is actually sinful in nature, but it gets far worse. Here's a list of other types of organizations who are also 501(c)(3) tax-exempt non-profits:

- The First Church of Satan [www.churchofsatan.org]
- Planned Parenthood (Baby-Killers) [www.plannedparenthood.org]
- Gay & Lesbian Advocates & Defenders [www.glad.org]
- Touchstone Local Council Covenant of the Goddess [www.tlcweb.org]

- The Secular Web (Anti-God Organization) [www. infidels.org]
- U.S. Conference of Catholic Bishops [www.uscb.org]
- QCinema: Gay & Lesbian Internation[al] Film Festival [www.qcinema.org]
- The Witches' Voice [www.witchvox.com]
- Church of Scientology [www.scientology.org]
- Satanist Cult of Cthulhu [www.cultofcthulhu.net]
- American Atheists [www.atheists.org]
- Mormon Church of Latter-Day Saints [www.lds.org]
- Pagan Druids of CedarLight Grove [www. cedarlightgrove.org]
- Islamic Society of Corona-Norco (Youth Camp) [www. coronamuslims.org]

These are the organizations your 501(c)(3) church, pastors, and deacons have chosen to associate with, and they need to come out from among them and be separate. Go visit some of these websites and see for yourself. These are just a few examples, but there are tens of *THOUSANDS* of these kinds of organizations flooding the 501(c)(3) incorporated (devil's) church. We are commanded *NOT* to get Christ's Church yoked up with these kinds of demonic organizations.[112]

You may have heard the phrase "ignorance of the law excuses not" (from the Latin *Ignorantia juris non excusat* or *ignorantia legis neminem excusat*). Silence on these matters will hold us in judgment of the wrongs that we do not stand against. Ignorance will not save us. Silence will not save us. Neither will ignorance redeem us of the sins that others commit in our clubhouse. It is time to stand together and be a glorious Church, without spot or wrinkle.

A House Divided

*No man can serve two masters: for either he will hate the one
and love the other; or he will hold to the one, and despise the other.
Ye cannot serve both God and mammon.*

MATTHEW 6:24

The 501(c)(3) has disarmed the Church and rendered it silent both
in the physical and the spiritual realm. Many churches now won't
speak up on important matters because they are afraid of losing their
501(c)(3) tax-exempt status. But the Lord is saying that we need to
choose a side. He is saying that the *Church* needs to choose a side.
Period.

Neutrality is not going to cut it, because that's lukewarm. The Lord
has said, "I will spew you out of My mouth if you are lukewarm" (cf.
Revelation 3:16). The Lord is looking for people who will stand up right
now and be biblically correct. It's funny; I wrote the 501(c)(3) prophecy
and only two months later, Trump said he was going to get rid of the
501(c)(3). This was right after I went public with it.

Whether he had seen my prophecy or not, I don't know. Honestly,
I doubt he had. I think he just picked up on it in the spirit because God
is calling his people out of the Babylonian systems, just as He told me
when He gave me this word in 2016:

He Spirit of God says, "There's a beast in the east that's trying
to arise that thinks he's the best, but I have one in the west that
will give him a godly surprise and take him down to the least.
For this beast that has risen is no surprise, for My Church is in a
Babylonian prison, come out of her or it will be to your demise!"

The Spirit of God says, "The chaos and clatter that the earth
is in, is directly related to the Babylonian box that the co-called

175

Church is in. For My earth is moaning and groaning for My sons and daughters to arise with bliss. Where is My Army that will send this beast back to the abyss? For how can you take on a beast when you're deaf, mute, and blind? For all beasts are ancient and old, and lurk about seeking an enemy whom they can steam roll. For this beast has no teeth and lurks in the brush, trying to lure you into an ambush. Do not attack until you come out of her, that Babylonian system, or you will fall prey and be decimated beyond comprehension."

The Spirit of God says, "For when My people realize the curse they are under, and come out, break the curse, then they will plunder. For as they come out of her with a mass exodus, there I will be, to restore her back to My Body and I as the head she will have power, authority, and unity again and the enemy shall fall as dead! For you wonder why the world is so perverse, it's because My Church has forsaken her first love and is under a curse. Come out of her now, don't walk but run and do not wait, before you cross the point of no return then it's too late. Come back to Me, come back to Me and make Me your first love I have dearly yearned, for some it's already too late, for they have not learned."

We talked about the counterfeit timeline in a previous chapter. The enemy has a timeline, and God has His. The problem with the 501(c)(3) church, because there's a demonic influence there, is that they are attached to the enemy's timeline.

And what we are hearing, as it pertains to the doomsday prophecies that run so rampant, are the plans of those powers that reign here on earth. But they are prophesying it as if these were God's own plans, and that's not the case.

While I was praying one day, God showed me something in my mind's eye. The Lord showed me a clock. One of His hands pointed to twelve o'clock, indicating His timeline. He then pointed to one o'clock with His other hand, which represented 1954, when the American Church first got off track. This meant that the Church was now attached to the enemy's timeline, because it was no longer on the timeline God had ordained. Then, as He stood there, pointing at both twelve and one, He told me that this signifies thirteen, which specifies rebellion. Between two elements—(1) the Church's enrollment in the 501(c)(3), which got them off track in the first place; and (2) its endorsing and prophesying the enemy's false timeline—the Lord was showing me that the Church is in a state of double rebellion.

You might remember that old saying, "Rangers, lead the way!" Well, it's the same way with the Church. The Church is supposed to lead the way. We are the ones who establish boundaries; we are the ones to provide direction. The Church is supposed to represent God's government. This can't be done when we're in a covenantal "government" contract with Ba'al in the spiritual realm. That's why Ba'al has been in power over this nation. The Lord Himself said we can't cast out Satan with Satan. How can we cast something out, when we're in covenant with it? There is a demonic influence over these 501(c)(3) churches because of the "who" they are in covenant with. They have become part of the Babylonian system, which cannot be anointed; therefore, neither can their *work* be anointed. Even when the people are in ministry for the right reasons, even when their message and their intent would normally be blessed by God—and regardless of how nice, flashy, or theologically correct their ministries are—it is fruitless if they are not *wholeheartedly* in covenant with God.

> *And Jesus went into the temple of God, and cast out all them that*
> *sold and bought in the temple, and overthrew the tables of the*
> *moneychangers, and the seats of them that sold doves. And said*
> *unto them, It is written, My house shall be called a house of prayer;*
> *but ye have made it a den of thieves.*
>
> MATTHEW 21:12–13

The Church was never intended to be a corporation. When we're incorporated, we are subject to the state. When we're subject to the state, Jesus is no longer the head of our ministry. This is why Jesus turned the tables over in the Temple, because it was not intended to be a place for moneychangers. It is a house of prayer. And a house of prayer should never be incorporated.

Ever.

God's house was not meant to be run like a business.

Peter Kershaw offers important insight on this matter:

Jesus did indeed say, "Render to Caesar the things that are Caesar's;" but that's only half the verse! Jesus went on to say, "and to God the things that are God's." The obvious question to be asked is at what time did Jesus place His church under the authority and jurisdiction of Caesar (the State)?

Mark 12:17 is the most brilliant teaching on lawful authority and legal jurisdiction that anyone has ever uttered. We can properly interpret Jesus' teaching in this way, "Don't render to Caesar the things that don't belong Caesar."

Only the "sovereign" (the supreme power) has the authority to impose a tax, and [H]e may do so only upon [H]is own citizen and subjects. Is the State sovereign over Jesus Christ and His body, the church? No, the civil government has no such lawful authority, biblically or constitutionally. If the civil government has the authority to tax the church, the church is a subordinate and a subject of the State.[113]

It is time for us to clean up God's house. The time for compromising "in the gray" is over. We need to decide if we are running a seat-warming club or an honest, sold-out ministry trying to reach the lost for Christ.

And if it seem evil unto you to serve the Lord,
choose you this day whom you will serve; whether the gods which
your father served that were on the other side of the flood,
or the gods of the Amorites, in whose land ye dwell:
but as for me and my house, we will serve the Lord.

JOSHUA 24:15

Another side effect of all this is the fact that this very issue has the Church preoccupied again with that intellect-against-intellect style of ungodly warfare. Confused? Simply Google-search the issue of churches and the 501(c)(3) and look at how many church blogs—*CHURCH BLOGS!*—are filled with stabby, jabby arguing among so-called believers about this matter. Personal insults are being hurled between fellow Christians, toward each other's integrity, and to their intelligence, name-calling, etc., all over this political matter—all the while these same individuals are arguing that politics don't belong in the Church.

Buyer's Remorse? Buyer Beware!

It may seem as though it would be easy enough to relinquish the 501(c)(3) tax status and regain our rights of speaking out, but this is simply not so. Once we have filed under 501(c)(3), we are considered a charitable organization, and cannot get out of the contract. We have, again, invited in jurisdiction to which we were previously not subject. Our assets now belong to the 501(c)(3) entity. In order to relinquish the tax exemption, we must surrender the 501(c)(3) assets. We can either turn them over to another tax-exempt charity ourselves (under tight parameters and with lengthy documentation), or we can fight this and the government can seize said assets and re-administer them among other 501(c)(3) organizations as it sees fit. Think of the abbreviated list of 501(c)(3)s earlier in this chapter. Can you imagine your church's assets being redistributed among these organizations? We can't leave a 501(c)(3) without losing everything. We lose it all. When we sign a deal with the devil, he always comes back for his dues.

Here is what the IRS has to say on this matter:

> Neither the Internal Revenue Code nor the Regulations make provision for voluntary relinquishment of exempt status by organizations that are not private foundations. The language of IRC 501(a) merely states that an organization "described in subsection (c)…shall be exempt from taxation under this subtitle." The use of the mandatory "shall" in IRC 501(a) has been construed by Chief Counsel to mean that so long as an organization does not violate the requirements of exemption neither the organization nor the Service may disregard such status. An organization's change of mind regarding its desire to be exempt is insufficient to overcome the mandatory language of IRC 501(a); only a change in operation or a proposed change in operation, *e.g.*, an organization amends its charter to provide for payment of dividends, can terminate its exempt status.

The previous paragraph makes it sound like a private foundation may have some other option of relinquishing tax-exempt status. But reading a little further, one can find the fine print on how a church specifically can withdraw from the 501(c)(3) status:

> A private foundation may voluntarily terminate its private foundation status under IRC 507(b)(1)(A) by distributing all its net assets to one or more public charities that are described in IRC 170(b)(1)(A)(i)-(vi) and have been public charities for 60 continuous months before the distribution of the private foundation's assets.…

A private foundation meets the requirement that it "distribute all of its net assets" within the meaning of IRC 507(b)(1)(A) only if it transfers "all of its right, title, and interest in and to all of its net assets" to one or more qualified public charities (Reg. 1.507-2(a)(7)).[114]

If churches were to begin speaking out, regardless of their 501(c)(3) agreement, would they then be reprimanded by having their tax-exempt status revoked? Possibly. Through certain loopholes, some attempts might be made to implement financial penalties or "back taxes." But this is assuming the church was subject to those taxes in the first place. Can you charge back taxes to an entity that was tax-exempt from the onset of our country? Perhaps the answer is to start speaking our minds, and let the chips fall where they may.

So what's a church to do? How can a church come out of the 501(c)(3) without losing everything? Unfortunately, there's no guarantee that this peaceful scenario will happen. But it is time to "count all things but loss for the excellency of the knowledge of Christ Jesus my Lord: for whom I have suffered the loss of all things, and do count them but dung, that I may win Christ, And be found in him, not having mine own righteousness" (Philippians 3:8–9).

The Church is the Body of Christ, not the assets it collects. Too many churches are far too preoccupied with attendance, numbers, money and tithes coming in, buildings, and programs. A building with pews and a pulpit is only that. Do these material things matter? Would we, the Church, gain the world to lose our soul?

All this being said, understand that the shape of the Church is changing! As I have said previously, we are going to start seeing more home churches, more street churches, more churches meeting in every kind of setting *besides* the traditional church building. Why is this? Because God is faithful, and where our "systems" have failed, He will raise us up! Get ready, because the Church of tomorrow is like nothing we have ever seen!

The Spiritual Backlash of the 501(c)(3)

Many think the Church doesn't belong in politics. Ask yourself: How's that working out for us so far? How are we supposed to be the moral compass of our country with our mouths shut? Every time there is a disaster, a terrorist attack, or fear of any kind amongst the people, where does everyone run for comfort and direction? Who do people turn to in calamity? They turn to God. They go to church. There is no room for saying the Church cannot be involved in politics. We're already in it, people—up to our elbows! We just need to untie our hands.

Take look at this timeline: The year 1954 was when the Bilderberg group, known as the New World Order, was established. Lyndon Johnson, a Freemason, set about to strip the Church of its power and authority. They devised a plan sponsored the attitude, "If we can't beat them, let's get them to join us."

The church was easily ensnared by the prospect of being able to pass tax deductions along to their contributors. Many, I'm sure, simply wanted to "live by the law of the land." Others sold out for the prospect of monetary gain. Regardless of which camp a church was in at that time, they readily signed on for this jurisdiction without a fight. Most probably didn't realize what they were really getting themselves into. Sadly, by the time churches fully understood the ramifications of the agreement, they were locked in.

So, as you can see, the political changes of 1954 got the ball rolling, and it has been snowballing ever since. That was more than sixty years ago, but the enemy is very patient.

How do you eat an elephant? One bite at a time.

About ten years after the Johnson Amendment, prayer was taken out of the schools. Where was the Church? Silent. They couldn't say a word, because they were *legally* bound by that agreement. Another decade went by, and *Roe vs. Wade* passed. Where was the Church? Silent.

It couldn't say anything...*legally*. That's on the Church's head, not on the general American population.

Look at every pertinent political change since then, especially considering how fast things escalate the more that time goes by since these changes began. The snowball grows daily. And where is the Church? *Still* silent. Are you tired of feeling powerless?

Do you think the government is corrupt? Why do you think that is? It's because the Church gave up. They quit being part of it. Think about it: Godly kings used to have godly advisors. Our government officials almost never do. Why? Because the Church has sold its seat. Because the Church has *forfeited* its role in government.

We're not just silent in the physical realm. We're every bit as silent in the spiritual realm also. For example, when *Roe vs. Wade* was passed, there were people who were out on the courthouse steps. I've heard them say, "I was screaming at the top of my lungs!" But sadly, they don't understand that legally, in the spiritual realm, if you are there representing a 501(c)(3) organization, your voice is not being heard in the spirit. It's not anointed. It's been taken away. You are in a covenant, bound in an agreement with the kingdom of darkness.

The Church's effectiveness is shackled to silence by the 501(c)(3). The Church has some serious repenting to do. Because these abortions—the blood of these murdered babies—is not just on "America's" hands. It's on the Church's hands. Again, allow me to emphasize: The bloodshed of these innocents lies not solely on America's hands; it is on the Church who stood by silently, selling out their voice for a tax exemption.

———

UPDATE: Trump Attempts to Repeal the Johnson Amendment
In February of 2017, at the National Prayer Breakfast, President Trump stated that he planned to "destroy the Johnson Amendment,"[115] explaining that religion was under threat and asserting his motivation to take action

to assist churches and religious institutions as it pertained to their rights to become politically involved. The president likewise stated, "We will not allow people of faith to be targeted, bullied or silenced anymore,"[116] then later on he stated that the government has "used the power of the state as a weapon against people of faith."[117]

While some claim that the president has completely done away with the 501(c)(3), this is not yet true, nor is it the case that he has eliminated the Johnson Amendment which prevents churches from being able to act out politically. What Trump *has* done, however, is loosen the limitations on churches imposed by the Johnson Amendment by signing an executive order that ensures leniency for religious organizations who have enacted their right to free speech: "The Secretary of the Treasury shall ensure, to the extent permitted by law, that the Department of the Treasury does not take any adverse action against any individual, house of worship, or other religious organization on the basis that such individual or organization speaks or has spoken about moral or political issues from a religious perspective, where speech of similar character has, consistent with law, not ordinarily been treated as participation or intervention in a political campaign on behalf of (or in opposition to) a candidate for public office by the Department of the Treasury."[118]

While the above language does not guarantee that the Johnson Amendment is going away just yet, it *does* render it less powerful than previously by limiting its ability to be enforced. Trump has made it clear from the beginning that his goal is to eliminate this law for the sake of free speech on behalf of those in religious leaderships.

On this matter, Trump stated: "No one should be censoring sermons or targeting pastors."[119]

Getting the Johnson Amendment repealed will take an act of Congress, and at this time, the volley regarding the matter rages on. Advocates for reversal maintain that churches should be allowed to speak out, while those in opposition to it state that churches should not endorse candidates, especially when they could in turn utilize favorable tax criteria as their reason for selecting governmental leaders to support. Others claim that allowing churches to speak out will turn the religious institution into a political arena, while yet another group begs for more political direction from the Church. The result of this ongoing debate manifests in the amendment being habitually tossed about within updates to each year's tax laws, but has yet to be permanently repealed.

In December of 2018, the U.S. House of Representatives voted to repeal the Johnson Amendment again.[120] While the House had previously included such an appeal in newly introduced tax provisions, the rescindment was removed before passing through the final legislative phases endorsed by U.S. Senate.

In an unexpected twist, the most recent bill approved by the House which included the revocation of the Johnson Amendment showed an indirect tie to pro-life preference as well: Language therein allows the parent of an unborn child to "recognize unborn children for the first time ever in the tax code, allowing parents, grandparents, or other relatives to open 529 educational savings accounts for an unborn child."[121]

As of now, the bill awaits the approval of the Senate, of which it will need the support of nine Senate Democrats in order to pass Congress.[122]

So What Do We Really Need?
A Church Without Spot or Wrinkle...

We, the Church, are supposed to be the spiritual and moral leaders of our country. Period. We, the Army of God. *We* are the ones who are supposed to show the way. We are the ones who tell our government which parameters and standards will be tolerated in society and which will not. The 501(c)(3) has reversed that role and rendered the Church powerless.

If my people...

In "The Lost Art of War," a word I received on December 12, 2016, the Holy Spirit told me:

The Spirit of God says, "Why are My people not repenting? You use generalized repentance, which has little to no effect, when you should be using target-focused repentance and prayer. You don't use target-focused repentance, because of your pride! Your haughty spirits and attitudes have caused you to fall into the enemy's pit. You're afraid of target-focused repentance, because you will have to admit there is fault with you and your congregation. By not repenting, this is an abomination. My people have lost the art of war, for any true warrior of Mine knows that waging an effective warfare starts with target-focused repentance and prayer."

The Spirit of God says, "Woe, Woe, Woe to you leaders that have led My people astray. You, who are cowardly and afraid of offending, have sacrificed My truth and My people on the altar of Mammon. Repent now or you will not come out of that pit, for truly you have received your reward and that's all you will get. You honor Me with your lips but your hearts are far from Me. Because of your pride and refusal to repent, there will be no hiding from this judgment. It's upon My Church, especially the leadership. Your big, fancy homes, clothes, and cars were made with money stained with innocent blood. This has allowed the enemy to come in on you like a flood. Even the Pharisees knew not to touch that money, but woe to you that continue to take it saying it's as sweet as honey. The blood, the blood which cries out to Me day and night, from the aborted babies to the murdering of My prophets. The blood is on My Church's hands, and yet no repentance? I am looking for My true love, My pure and spotless bride, and it grieves Me her garments are stained because of pride. Where is she? Where is she, My true love, I can no longer wait, My judgment is upon you. Repent and come back, before it's too late."

It is time for us to invite a habitation of the Holy Spirit into our lives—our churches—and by doing so, our government. Not a scheduled, stale, calendar-marked, preplanned, "revival," constituting more nights per week preplanned by the same, pew-warming clubhouse members. We need a real, radical, sweeping, all-out, sold-out surrender to God that overtakes everything.

Everything!

> *For I am jealous over you with godly jealousy:*
> *for I have espoused you to one husband, t*
> *hat I may present you as a chaste virgin to Christ.*
> 2 CORINTHIANS 11:2

Remember when I said that the Church is bleeding out? It is time to perform spiritual triage. It's time for a role reversal. It's time for God's government to be setting the boundaries for what is and is not acceptable in our land. It's time for the remnant to emerge and begin to take ground...*and hold it.*

What does God want in a church? Purity and unwavering devotion! It's time for the church to quit praying "generally." We need to repent "specifically." Target-focused. He is waiting for His bride, His church without spot or wrinkle.

Awake, Church! Clean the temple and prepare, oh Army of God!

> *Wherefore he saith, Awake thou that sleepest,*
> *and arise from the dead,*
> *and Christ shall give thee light.*
> EPHESIANS 5:14

Taking Ground!

The most important message I can leave you with is this: Take ground, and hold it at all costs! As I have explained, God has given me the word that likens modern-day America to the hub of D-Day activity. We have a great and mighty work ahead of us! Each and every one of us is placed *for such a time as this*. The Church has a terrible habit of taking ground and then backing off when pressure subsides. This leaves territory unclaimed and vulnerable to further invasion and habitation.

> *When the unclean spirit is gone out of a man, he walketh through dry places, seeking rest, and findeth none. Then he saith, I will return into my house from whence I came out; and when he is come, he findeth it empty, swept, and garnished. Then goeth he, and taketh with himself seven other spirits more wicked than himself, and they enter in and dwell there: and the last state of that man is worse than the first, Even so shall it be also unto this wicked generation.*
>
> MATTHEW 12:43–45

Understand that in the spirit realm, battles have a location just as a physical battle has a tangible location. Our battle rages on in the spirit realm, against supernatural forces and in spiritual places. Army of God, know your enemy, and know how to prepare. Understand what it really means to take ground and hold it, and understand that when I say this, I am talking about spiritual warfare.

> *Put on the whole armour of God, that ye may be able to stand against the wiles of the devil. For we wrestle not against flesh and blood, but against principalities, against powers, against the rulers of the darkness of this world, against spiritual wickedness in high places. Wherefore take unto you the whole armour of God, that ye may be able to withstand in the evil day, and having done all, to stand.*
>
> EPHESIANS 6:11–13

Take Ground and Hold It

Think about all the things that we do not follow through with. Many of us are good in a crisis, but who can be found at the scene, still running maintenance on a situation long after emergency intervention has been performed? Even in our everyday lives we take ground, only to become sloppy and lazy again in the honeymoon phase of triumph.

We diet, just to accomplish our goal weight, and then load up on cake and gain the pounds back. We save money, just to "splurge" on something that then leaves us without savings again. We organize, just to turn around the next day and begin the same cluttery piles on our desk. We purchase home-improvement materials that sit in the garage and collect dust. We bring home supplies for starting a new hobby only to leave them on a shelf and later donate them—still in the package—to a thrift store because we have given up on ever making time to follow through. We make new "household rules" we don't follow up on. We pay for gym memberships we don't use. We buy cookbooks we don't even open. We buy vitamins we don't take. We set bedtimes, budgets, schedules, maintenance plans, even boundaries in relationships and friendships…and then completely disregard them when it's time for following through.

But worse, we do this *spiritually*. We tell people we will pray for them, and then forget to do it. We say we'll attend church and never get around to it. We don't make time to read our Bibles or pray the way we should. We turn a blind eye to those in need and say that we will do something about their need tomorrow.

In a crisis, we band together for the good of the issue we are facing. We pray, fast, encourage each other, attend special church services, give to emergency funds, and sometimes even protest or take visibly public actions to see our goals achieved. But once our goal is accomplished, we retreat to where we were before the calamity hit, leaving ground uncovered and vulnerable to reinvasion by the enemy.

It's important to understand that in the spirit world there are territories wherein these things occur. Each battle has a location in the supernatural realm. Imagine a country that is resisting a takeover by the army of an opposing country. The defending country will fight and do battle for days and nights on end until it has finally gained enough ground that the enemy withdraws. Would that country then just leave? Would it abandon the area its soldiers fought so hard to defend?

Why do we do this as Christians?

Consider what the Holy Spirit whispered to me in the "Operation Let My People Go" word of July 8, 2016:

The Spirit of God says, "When Donald Trump is elected, a sign will be given. The earth shall shake and quake because of who I have selected. It's a shift, a shift in the power structure that is taking place and another sign will be given when it falls without grace. A lightning strike and a great wind shall topple the so-called great monument, and they will not be able to mend. It will be a sign that the Luciferian reign and ungodly powers are coming to an end. I have had it with time and truth that bends. When it topples and shatters the capstone the builders accepted will be exposed for all to see and the one they rejected, who is Me. For these ungodly powers I, the Lord will expose! From the Illuminati to the Cabal, they are beginning to decompose. For those that speak of myths of wrath to come are creating fanaticism, and they will go down to the abyss with a cataclysm."

The Spirit of God says, "The timeline, the counterfeit timeline that they have used, you shall see it and how it's been abused. For the counterfeit timeline that they have used to lead My people astray, will be exposed and seen because My remnant people have prayed. You people who speak with time and truth that bend, thinking you have encircled My body and sealed them in, hoping it's now their end. For you are saying they are no longer a threat for they accepted a truth that bends. Woe to you, for you forgot about My remnant and that's My surprise, and now it's your end and it shall be your demise! For the counterfeit spiritual compass that is pulling and magnetizing My people off course as it be, will be turned back by My true Army, and pointed true north, and back to Me."

The Spirit of God says, "Woe to those that have tried to enslave My people, for now I will topple your so-called steeple. It has stood for so long, that beast of old called Babylon! For this new world order that seeks to destroy, forgot about My true Army that is being deployed. My Army, rise up with a shout, for this evil reign is being exposed with clout. My Army, My Army, rise up and take on this beast, and I the Lord God will take him down to the least. For this beast is roaring trying to intimidate, through assassinations, division, and hate. Rise up! It's time to battle against this beast with extreme prejudice and you will terminate!"

"Your Supreme Commander, God"

No Turning Back

As I mentioned earlier in the book, when I retired from firefighting, I threw away all of my work-related paraphernalia. I had my wife bring in a trash bag, and we packed it all up together and hauled it out. Some may think this is a sad way to end a career that someone dreamed of since childhood, but for me it was a purging. It was a mile marker between two roads in my life, a solid sign that one journey had ended and a new one was beginning.

Remember in the D-Day chapter, when I mentioned the pilots who hesitated and dropped their bombs almost a mile away from their target? When God calls you to action, it's time to move. Don't wait, and don't look back.

> *And he said unto another, Follow me. But he said, Lord, suffer me first to go and bury my father. Jesus said to him, Let the dead bury their dead: but go thou and preach the kingdom of God.*
> Luke 9:59–60

When Jesus said to this man that he could not go back and bury his dead, He was telling him that it was time to go without hesitating: no turning back.

When You Pray

I want to remind you of the importance of target-focused repentance and prayer. When you pray, it's not enough to just pray generically.

Think about what would happen if you went into a restaurant and said to the waitress, "I'll take some dinner." It's a humorous idea, but I would imagine if you were to try that, she would laugh, then bring you a menu and ask you to be more specific.

The Lord told me, "Mark, the prayer and repentance My people are using is too generalized." An example of this is: "Lord, forgive me for my sins." That is a generalized prayer of repentance. Now, make no mistake, this prayer, spoken in sincerity to the Lord from a desperate sinner, is plenty to open the floodgates of God's saving grace within one's life. But for believers to pray so indiscriminately within the mature stages of their walk with the Lord, it means that they are missing out on much of the power of prayer. More mature believers should be in tune with their own weakness enough to pray, for example, "God, please strengthen me against the sin of pride today. Please help me to hold every thought captive to Your will, as I go through this day setting an example of Christ in me."

Consider this: The Bible says that where two or more are agreed, God is there in the midst of them. *Just two*! And, even further, what they bind on earth, using their prayer words, will be bound in heaven. What is let loose on earth is likewise let loose in heaven. This is how powerful our prayer words are! Can you *really grasp* what I'm telling you? You have an audience with the *very Maker of this universe* every time you are in agreement in prayer. And He has promised in His Word that when you pray and bind or let loose things here on earth, the forces of heaven make it so in the spiritual realm. Talk about words that invoke authority!

Imagine if God, Himself, were standing physically in front of you right now. Picture that you can see Him with your eyes, touch Him with your fingertips, and hear His audible words with your ears. Now, remembering that what you say to Him will unleash ultimate power from heaven behind it, what do you say to Him? Is it a general statement or two? Or is it specific, empowered conversation?

When we pray, we have to endow our prayers with spoken word. We have to ask God in detail for what we are binding in heaven, and what is being let loose.

> *Verily I say unto you, Whatsoever ye shall bind on earth*
> *shall be bound in heaven: and whatsoever ye shall loose on*
> *earth shall be loosed in heaven. Again I say unto you, That*
> *if two of you shall agree on earth as touching any thing*
> *that they shall ask, it shall be done for them of my Father*
> *which is in heaven. For where two or three are gathered*
> *together in my name, there am I in the midst of them.*
> MATTHEW 18:18–20

We have to say explicitly what we are hoping to see, what we are repenting for, or what miracles we are asking God to bring. When we pray this way, we are lining up heavenly powers to focus on precise targets within the spirit realm. It's important that, when we are praying or repenting, we envision our purpose, laser designate our "target," and pray specifically. Our specific prayer is the "smart bomb" that will always hit the mark!

Calling the Remnant

Who is going to make changes happen now? I hate to be the bearer of bad news, but I don't think it will be the "traditional" Church. It will be the *remnant*. As times ahead change, it will be the job of those within the remnant to step forward and answer the call that God is placing on their lives. It's important that we do not presume these roles for ourselves or chase after them for our own reasons. As I said before: Man qualifies the *called*; God qualifies the *chosen*. God will be choosing the next round of leaders in this nation. We must prayerfully wait for God, Himself, to instruct us on where exactly that places us.

But understand that if we stand together in prayer and honest willingness to do God's will and surrender wholeheartedly to His work, nothing is impossible. Take a look at the election of 2016! It was not necessarily the Church that pulled that off. It was the Army of God.

It was the remnant.

That's who pulled this off. And, it's only the beginning!

The transformation is taking place. The remnant is waking up, and the winds of change are upon us. Begin today. Seize this moment, it's the only one you can really be sure that you have. Take the Gospel to the people. Don't wait for people to come to you; *you must be the one to go to them.* Think of what the Army of God can do with all the power of heaven behind us!

Everywhere you go, keep the Gospel right there. Take it with you. Get up off the church pews and reinstate the Great Commission!

Preach the Gospel right there on the street corner. Take it to the marketplace. Carry it to work. Whisper it through the library. Boast it loudly in the locker room. Hit the streets, take ground...*and hold that ground.*

Remember the Code of Conduct

God has called you, His Army, to fight. Soldiers are just that, 24/7. But while we were called to fight a noble battle, we were absolutely *not* called to fight in every battle we come across. We are not to be at war with each other. It is important that you remember the mission, and remember that there are certain instructions He is initiating you to follow. Every nation's army has a code of conduct, and the Army of God is no exception.

Remember that the enemy would love to bully you with his timeline. Don't give in! God is the orchestrator of *all* of time, and only He will decide when we are to lay down our arms. Don't stop fighting! Quitting is not an option. Getting others to resign is committing spiritual treason!

Do not take on ungodly warfare between each other. God does not want His army divided by pettiness or argumentativeness. He wants a glorious Church, an Army of mission-minded soldiers. Do not fight each other using your intellect.

Keep yourself pure and focused on the battle. I've never consumed alcohol, smoked, or taken drugs. I always felt like the Lord wanted me to stay away from those activities, just as the angel told Sampson's mother that he would be sanctified as a Nazarite from birth because his destiny was so great. *You, too, have a great destiny ahead of you.* Whatever it is the Lord has told you to refrain from on a personal level, keep yourself pure and holy as a living sacrifice unto the Lord so that He can bless your role in the upcoming transformation here on earth.

Be a Glorious Church

The face of the Church is changing. Be flexible, and willing to change as God instructs. But follow His voice. Let go of the trivial things that have become obstacles for the traditional Church: money, attendance, programs, statistics, political correctness, etc. Understand that our battle is not in the physical realm and material things are a distraction.

One megachurch—just one!—if dumped on a street on a Sunday morning, could transform a city overnight if the hearts of that congregation were passionate toward such a goal! Imagine the lost who would be reached for Christ if the Church were to refocus its energy. The Church may need to become adaptable, and nomadic. Believers must be ready to rise to the occasion.

Revival is in the air! It may be a hard concept to grasp, but this isn't actually about politics. It's about the habitation of the Holy Spirit throughout this land. It's about our country transforming into a zone where the Spirit of the Lord can move freely throughout the people again. It's about the need to redirect the Church's energy to be more effective with both the ground that lies unclaimed and/or the ground that has been taken.

We can have a football stadium filled with Christians holding a "revival," but without true residence of the Holy Spirit, where will it get us? Nowhere. "Revivals" come and go. I want to have a permanent indwelling of the Holy Spirit. Take that same football stadium of believers and empower them with the Holy Spirit, and we've got an Army for Christ. *Literally.* We have an invasion force.

It's time to get out of our comfort zones. We must be ready and willing to march, to leave the familiarity of our four walls and venture into the unknown for Christ.

This is how I interpret the New Testament Church: Jesus sent its members out. They were not in one geographical location. They were fluid. They were mobile, constantly moving. If Jesus is in you, and you are in Him, *you are* the Gospel. How do you share that Gospel sitting in four walls of the Church? It's time to stop waiting for people to come to us. We *have* to start going to the people. This is the very essence of the Great Commission.

Good Things Are Coming!

Our future is very bright. The change that has begun will continue if God's people will keep uniting in prayer and focusing on the mission.

Being confident of this very thing,
that he which hath begun a good work in
you will perform it until the day of Jesus Christ.
PHILIPPIANS 1:6

God has indeed begun a good work in our world, our country, and our Church. He will be faithful to complete it as His Word says.

Army of God, awaken! Open your eyes and your ears to the Lord, Himself. Get rid of religion, set aside legalism, and focus on the Lord. Don't be distracted by obstacles. Concentrate on the mission…

And once again, *what* is the mission?

Take ground for the Kingdom—and hold it—at all costs!

God is ordering His people to clean up, and right now we're wearing soiled garments. He is coming back for a pure and spotless bride, so come out of the Babylonian systems and strive for target-focused prayer and repentance.

Never forget that *we* are the Gospel. It's time to start moving. We've been stagnant for too long. We *cannot* reach the lost just sitting in a pew.

We have got to take the fight to the enemy and stop listening to the doom and gloom that surrounds us. Christians are not the weak, outnumbered, or powerless folks that the world around tries to tell us we are, and it's high time we begin to believe in our power as God's Army. The days of silence and complacency are over. No more hesitating! It's time to light up our world with a Holy Fire!

Remember that even though God has anointed Donald Trump for such a time as this, he is still *just a man*, called by God to do a work. But he is not the only person called by God. You are also a part of this, and so am I. We are in this together as the body of Christ, and we are about to see amazing things! The seeds that America has planted since its beginning are about to come to fruition, and we are among the fortunate, blessed generation that will be allowed to witness this triumphant day!

Remember: No matter your past, educational history, status, health, or any other circumstances in your life, if you will take a stand—if you will join in God's Army just as you are—God *can and will* use you. HE qualifies the chosen. Start today! Move forward and begin to take ground and hold ground at all costs. You are a part of the amazing victory that is coming our way. Put on the armor of God and join the fight.

Onward, Christian Soldiers!

———

UPDATE: Time Is Up for Those Who Are Corrupt

In the prophetic word by the same title that Mark Taylor shared with the world written in 2015, he declared, "Time is up for those who are corrupt!" He stated that those in high positions of power who have used their advantages to deceive American people would be exposed, and the dark deeds carried out in secret would be brought to light.

On October 10, 2016, during his presidential campaign, Trump stated: "If I win, I am going to instruct my attorney general to get a special prosecutor to look into [Hillary Clinton's] situation [regarding missing emails], because there has never been so many lies, so much deception."[123] He later accused Clinton of bleaching and deleting 33,000 emails in response to a congressional subpoena. Under Title 18 U.S. Code, Sec. 2071, Clinton could be charged with destroying State Department evidence, a felony which can carry up to three years of prison time.[124]

However, it would appear that mere emails are only the beginning of the trouble surrounding certain figures in Washington, D.C. In April of 2018, eleven House Republicans "signed a joint letter to Attorney General Jeff Sessions calling for the criminal prosecution of Hillary Clinton and a variety of other Obama administration appointees, career FBI officials, and even Trump appointee Dana Boente, who is currently the FBI's general counsel."[125]

As investigations heat up within proximity of the White House, Mark reminds us to be in prayer for our nation and our president. Indeed, the time draws near for those who are corrupt to be brought to justice. Mark believes that there will soon be indictments within Washington, D.C. along with prosecutions before military tribunals, and states that the vast majority of governmental changes still lay ahead of us. He prompts the Body of Christ to be united and steadfast as we approach these tumultuous times, and encourages us to remember that when the world around us falters, God is in control.

"I will lift up mine eyes unto the hills, from whence cometh my help. My help cometh from the Lord, which made heaven and earth. He will not suffer thy foot to be moved: he that keepeth thee will not slumber" Psalm 121:1–3.

———

Notes

1. "Pharaoh's Final Quarter-Mile Carried Him to Triple Crown," June 9, 2015, ESPN News Online, last accessed February 28, 2017, http://www.espn.com/horse-racing/story/_/id/13043616/ pharoah-final-belmont-quarter-mile-faster-secretariat.

2. Johnny Enlow, "Triple Crown Winner American Pharoah? Is This Good or Bad?" June 18, 2015, The ElijahList Online, last accessed March 6, 2017, http://www.elijahlist.com/words/display_word.html?ID=14839.

3. "Norman Cota, Overlooked Hero of D-Day (And the Next)," Updated from the 2014 version, New England Historical Society Online, last accessed March 6, 2017, http://www.newenglandhistoricalsociety.com/ norman-cota-overlooked-hero-d-day-next-day/.

4. Socrates, "Our lives are but specks of dust falling through the fingers of time. Like sands of the hourglass, so are the days of our lives," Quote Fancy Online, Accessed February 12, 2019, https://quotefancy.com/ quote/908553/Socrates-Our-lives-are-but-specks-of-dust-falling-through-the-fingers-of-time-Like-sands.

5. Katharine Lee Bates, "America, the Beautiful," 1913, USA Flag Site Online, last accessed March 22, 2017, http://www.usa-flag-site.org/song-lyrics/ america/.

6. Matthew Grimson, "Port Arthur Massacre: The Shooting Spree that Changed Australia's Gun Laws," April 28, 2016, NBC News Online,

last accessed March 23, 2017, http://www.nbcnews.com/news/world/
port-arthur-massacre-shooting-spree-changed-australia-gun-laws-n396476.

7. Warren Fiske, "NRA Weakly Claims that Clinton Said Gun
   Confiscation Is 'Worth Considering,'" October 17, 2016, Politifact
   Virginia Online, last accessed March 23, 2017, http://www.politifact.
   com/virginia/statements/2016/oct/17/national-rifle-association/
   nra-weakly-claims-clinton-said-gun-confiscation-wo/.

8. John R. Lott, "Four Ways Hillary Clinton Will Work to End Gun
   Ownership as President," June 6, 2016, Fox News Opinion Online, last
   accessed March 23, 2017, http://www.foxnews.com/opinion/2016/06/06/
   four-ways-president-hillary-clinton-will-work-to-end-gun-ownership.html.

9. Dinesh D'Souza, "The Corruption of Hillary Clinton,"
   November 28, 2016, Frontpage Mag Online, last accessed
   March 23, 2017, http://www.frontpagemag.com/fpm/264968/
   corruption-hillary-clinton-frontpagemagcom.

10. Bedard, Paul, "Trump's list: 289 accomplishments in just 20 months,
    'relentless' promise-keeping," October, 12, 2018, The Washington
    Examiner, last accessed January 30, 2019, https://www.washingtonexaminer.
    com/washington-secrets/trumps-list-289-accomplishments-in-just-20-
    months-relentless-promise-keeping.

11. Bedard, Paul, "Trump's list: 289 accomplishments in just 20 months,
    'relentless' promise-keeping," October, 12, 2018, The Washington
    Examiner, last accessed January 30, 2019, https://www.washingtonexaminer.
    com/washington-secrets/trumps-list-289-accomplishments-in-just-20-
    months-relentless-promise-keeping

12. Jeremy Diamond, "Trump Orders Construction of Border Wall, Boosts
    Deportation Force," January 25, 2017, CNN Politics Online, last
    accessed March 23, 2017, http://www.cnn.com/2017/01/25/politics/
    donald-trump-build-wall-immigration-executive-orders/.

13. Ibid.

14. Trump, Donald. "Trump calls out Russia for violating nuclear treaty,"
    House Chamber; The State of the Union, CNN Politics Online, February

6, 2019, last accessed February 8, 2019, https://www.cnn.com/videos/politics/2019/02/06/trump-state-of-the-union-2019-russia-inf-nuclear-treaty-sot-vpx.cnn.

15. Trump, Donald. "Trump calls out Russia for violating nuclear treaty," House Chamber; The State of the Union, CNN Politics Online, February 6, 2019, last accessed February 8, 2019, https://www.cnn.com/videos/politics/2019/02/06/trump-state-of-the-union-2019-russia-inf-nuclear-treaty-sot-vpx.cnn.

16. Superville, Darlene, "Trump signs $700 billion military budget into law," PBS New Hour Online, December 12, 2017, last accessed January 30, 2019, https://www.pbs.org/newshour/politics/trump-signs-700-billion-military-budget-into-law.

17. Borger, Julian, "Donald Trump signs executive order to keep Guantánamo Bay open," The Guardian Online, January 30, 2018, last accessed January 30, 2019, https://www.theguardian.com/us-news/2018/jan/30/guantanamo-bay-trump-signs-executive-order-to-keep-prison-open.

18. Graves, Allison, "Trump-O-Meter: Keep Guantánamo Bay Detention Center open," Politifact Online January 16, 2017, last accessed February 8, 2019, https://www.politifact.com/truth-o-meter/promises/trumpometer/promise/1373/keep-guantanamo-bay-detention-center-open/.

19. Wolf, Richard, "Supreme Court upholds President Trump's travel ban against majority-Muslim countries," USA Today Online, June 26, 2018, last accessed January 30, 2019, https://www.usatoday.com/story/news/politics/2018/06/26/supreme-court-upholds-president-trump-immigration-travel-ban/701110002/.

20. Higgins, Tucker, "Supreme Court rules that Trump's travel ban is constitutional," CNBC Online, June 28, 2018, last accessed February 8, 2019, https://www.cnbc.com/2018/06/26/supreme-court-rules-in-trump-muslim-travel-ban-case.html.

21. Higgins, Tucker, "Supreme Court rules that Trump's travel ban is constitutional," CNBC Online, June 28, 2018, last accessed February 8, 2019, https://www.cnbc.com/2018/06/26/supreme-court-rules-in-trump-muslim-travel-ban-case.html.

22. De Luce, Dan & Ainsley, Julia, "Trump admin intentionally slowing FBI vetting of refugees, ex-officials say," NBC News Online, August 24, 2018, last accessed January 31, 2019, https://www.nbcnews.com/politics/ immigration/trump-admin-intentionally-slowing-fbi-vetting-refugees-ex-officials-say-n903346.

23. Alvarado, Beatriz, "Construction on President Donald Trump's border wall to begin in February," Caller Times, November 2, 2018, last accessed January 31, 2019, https:// www.caller.com/story/news/texasregion/2018/11/02/ construction-trumps-border-wall-begin-february/1861864002/.

24. Alvarado, Beatriz, "Construction on President Donald Trump's border wall to begin in February," Caller Times, November 2, 2018, last accessed January 31, 2019, https:// www.caller.com/story/news/texasregion/2018/11/02/ construction-trumps-border-wall-begin-february/1861864002/.

25. Alvarado, Beatriz, "Construction on President Donald Trump's border wall to begin in February," Caller Times, November 2, 2018, last accessed January 31, 2019, https:// www.caller.com/story/news/texasregion/2018/11/02/ construction-trumps-border-wall-begin-february/1861864002/.

26. Alvarado, Beatriz, "Construction on President Donald Trump's border wall to begin in February," Caller Times, November 2, 2018, last accessed January 31, 2019, https:// www.caller.com/story/news/texasregion/2018/11/02/ construction-trumps-border-wall-begin-february/1861864002/.

27. Da Silva, Chantal, "Is Donald Trump's Border Wall Already Being Built? Construction Begins In Texas On 4-Mile-Long Section Costing $22 Million," Newsweek Online, September 24, 2018, last accessed January 31, 2019, https://www.newsweek.com/donald-trumps-border-wall-already-being-built-construction-begins-texas-4-1135603.

28. Bedard, Paul, "Trump's list: 289 accomplishments in just 20 months, 'relentless' promise-keeping," The Washington Examiner Online, October

12, 2018, last accessed January 31, 2019, https://www.washingtonexaminer.com/washington-secrets/trumps-list-289-accomplishments-in-just-20-months-relentless-promise-keeping.

29. Attorney General, Department of Justice: Office of Public Affairs, "Attorney General Sessions Announces New Measures to Fight Transnational Organized Crime," US Department of Justice Official Website, October 23, 2017, last accessed February 8, 2019, https://www.justice.gov/opa/pr/attorney-general-sessions-announces-new-measures-fight-transnational-organized-crime.

30. Bedard, Paul, "Trump's list: 289 accomplishments in just 20 months, 'relentless' promise-keeping," The Washington Examiner Online, October 12, 2018, last accessed January 31, 2019, https://www.washingtonexaminer.com/washington-secrets/trumps-list-289-accomplishments-in-just-20-months-relentless-promise-keeping.

31. Bedard, Paul, "Trump's list: 289 accomplishments in just 20 months, 'relentless' promise-keeping," The Washington Examiner Online, October 12, 2018, last accessed January 31, 2019, https://www.washingtonexaminer.com/washington-secrets/trumps-list-289-accomplishments-in-just-20-months-relentless-promise-keeping.

32. Ahmed, Azam, "How El Chapo Was Finally Captured, Again," The New York Times Online, January 16, 2016, last accessed February 8, 2019, https://www.nytimes.com/2016/01/17/world/americas/mexico-el-chapo-sinaloa-sean-penn.html.

33. Sanchez, Ray, "'El Chapo' Guzman pleads not guilty in US to 17 counts," CNN Online, January 20, 2017, last accessed February 2019, https://www.cnn.com/2017/01/20/us/el-chapo-guzman-extradition/index.html.

34. Moghe, Sonia, "El Chapo jury deliberations will stretch into a second week. Here's why jurors may be taking their time," CNN Online, February 8, 2019, last accessed February 8, 2019, https://www.cnn.com/2019/02/08/us/el-chapo-guzman-trial-jurors-deliberation-week/index.html.

35. Coffman, Keith, "El Chapo, if convicted, would likely do time in 'Supermax' prison," Reuters Online, January 21, 2017, last

accessed February 8, 2019, https://www.reuters.com/article/us-mexico-crime-chapo-prison-idUSKBN1550E0.

36. Coffman, Keith, "El Chapo, if convicted, would likely do time in 'Supermax' prison," Reuters Online, January 21, 2017, last accessed February 8, 2019, https://www.reuters.com/article/us-mexico-crime-chapo-prison-idUSKBN1550E0.

37. Azar, Alex, "Trump administration making progress in fight against opioid epidemic: HHS Secretary," USA Today Online, September 19, 2018, last accessed February 8, 2019, https://www.usatoday.com/story/opinion/2018/09/19/donald-trump-opioid-crisis-epidemic-addiction-nalaxone-heroine-column/1347574002/.

38. Azar, Alex, "Trump administration making progress in fight against opioid epidemic: HHS Secretary," USA Today Online, September 19, 2018, last accessed February 8, 2019, https://www.usatoday.com/story/opinion/2018/09/19/donald-trump-opioid-crisis-epidemic-addiction-nalaxone-heroine-column/1347574002/.

39. Bedard, Paul, "Trump's list: 289 accomplishments in just 20 months, 'relentless' promise-keeping," The Washington Examiner Online, October 12, 2018, last accessed January 31, 2019, https://www.washingtonexaminer.com/washington-secrets/trumps-list-289-accomplishments-in-just-20-months-relentless-promise-keeping.

40. Fritze, John & Shesgreen, Deirdre, "Trump implores world leaders at United Nations to confront 'scourge' of drug addiction," USA Today Online, September 24, 2018, last accessed January 31, 2019, https://www.usatoday.com/story/news/politics/2018/09/24/donald-trump-united-nations-must-confront-confront-scourge-drugs/1408197002/.

41. Joseph Dutton, "What Trump's 'Energy Independent' US Would Mean for the Rest of the World," November 22, 2016, Business Insider Online, The Conversation, last accessed March 23, 2017, http://www.businessinsider.com/trumps-energy-independent-us-impact-on-the-rest-of-the-world-2016-11.

42. DiChristopher, Tom, "Trump's year in OPEC tweets: How the president

deflected blame for rising prices," December 4, 2018, last accessed February 7, 2019, https://www.cnbc.com/2018/12/04/an-annotated-guide-to-trumps-2018-opec-tweets.html.

43. DiChristopher, Tom, "Trump's year in OPEC tweets: How the president deflected blame for rising prices," December 4, 2018, last accessed February 7, 2019, https://www.cnbc.com/2018/12/04/an-annotated-guide-to-trumps-2018-opec-tweets.html.

44. "Trump Just Achieved What Every President Since Nixon Had Promised: Energy Independence," Investors Business Daily Online, December 7, 2018, last accessed February 7, 2019, https://www.investors.com/politics/editorials/energy-independence-trump/.

45. "Trump Just Achieved What Every President Since Nixon Had Promised: Energy Independence," Investors Business Daily Online, December 7, 2018, last accessed February 7, 2019, https://www.investors.com/politics/editorials/energy-independence-trump/.

46. "Trump Just Achieved What Every President Since Nixon Had Promised: Energy Independence," Investors Business Daily Online, December 7, 2018, last accessed February 7, 2019, https://www.investors.com/politics/editorials/energy-independence-trump/.

47. "Trump Just Achieved What Every President Since Nixon Had Promised: Energy Independence," Investors Business Daily Online, December 7, 2018, last accessed February 7, 2019, https://www.investors.com/politics/editorials/energy-independence-trump/.

48. Gardner, Timothy, "U.S. coal exports soar, in boost to Trump energy agenda, data shows," Reuters Online, July 27, 2017, last accessed January 30, 2019. https://www.reuters.com/article/us-usa-coal-exports/u-s-coal-exports-soar-in-boost-to-trump-energy-agenda-data-shows-idUSKBN1AD0DU.

49. Bastasch, Micheal, "Trump Unveils Proposal for Oil and Gas Drilling in ANWR," Daily Caller, December 20, 2018, last accessed January 30, 2019, https://da.ilycaller.com/2018/12/20/anwr-alaska-interior-oil-drilling/.

50. Labott, Elise & Diamond, Jeremy, "Trump administration approves

Keystone XL pipeline," CNN Online, March 24, 2017, last accessed January 30, 2019, https://www.cnn.com/2017/03/23/politics/keystone-xl-pipeline-trump-approve/index.html.

51. "Benefits of Keystone XL," Global Energy Institute, 2019, last accessed February 7, 2019, https://www.globalenergyinstitute.org/benefits-keystone-xl.

52. "Benefits of Keystone XL," Global Energy Institute, 2019, last accessed February 7, 2019, https://www.globalenergyinstitute.org/benefits-keystone-xl.

53. Eilperin, Juliet & Dennis, Brady, "Trump administration to approve final permit for Dakota Access pipeline," The Washington Post, February 7, 2017, https://www.washingtonpost.com/news/energy-environment/wp/2017/02/07/trump-administration-to-approve-final-permit-for-dakota-access-pipeline/?utm_term=.5195c214d80a. Last accessed January 30, 2019.

54. Malik, Naureen, "U.S. Becomes a Net Gas Exporter for the First Time in 60 Years," Bloomberg Online, January 10, 2018, last accessed January 30, 2019, https://www.bloomberg.com/news/articles/2018-01-10/u-s-became-a-net-gas-exporter-for-the-first-time-in-60-years.

55. "Donald Trump says he might sign back up to a revamped Paris accord," The Guardian, January 27, 2018, last accessed January 30, 2019, https://www.theguardian.com/us-news/2018/jan/28/donald-trump-says-he-might-sign-back-up-to-a-revamped-paris-accord.

56. "Fact check: Trump's Paris Agreement withdrawal announcement," Climate Analytics Online, 2019, last accessed February 7, 2019, https://climateanalytics.org/briefings/fact-check-trumps-paris-agreement-withdrawal-announcement/.

57. Bedard, Paul, "Trump's list: 289 accomplishments in just 20 months, 'relentless' promise-keeping," The Washington Examiner Online, October 12, 2018, last accessed January 31, 2019, https://www.washingtonexaminer.com/washington-secrets/trumps-list-289-accomplishments-in-just-20-months-relentless-promise-keeping.

58. Trump, Donald, "Trump Administration Accomplishments," The White House Official Website, last accessed January 30, 2019. https://www.whitehouse.gov/trump-administration-accomplishments/.

59. Trump, Donald, "Trump Administration Accomplishments," The White House Official Website, last accessed January 30, 2019. https://www.whitehouse.gov/trump-administration-accomplishments/.

60. Bedard, Paul, "Trump's list: 289 accomplishments in just 20 months, 'relentless' promise-keeping," The Washington Examiner Online, October 12, 2018, last accessed January 31, 2019, https://www.washingtonexaminer.com/washington-secrets/trumps-list-289-accomplishments-in-just-20-months-relentless-promise-keeping.

61. Bedard, Paul, "Trump's list: 289 accomplishments in just 20 months, 'relentless' promise-keeping," The Washington Examiner Online, October 12, 2018, last accessed January 31, 2019, https://www.washingtonexaminer.com/washington-secrets/trumps-list-289-accomplishments-in-just-20-months-relentless-promise-keeping.

62. Cox, Jeff, "There are more jobs than people out of work, something the American economy has never experienced before," CNBC Online, June 5, 2018, last accessed February 7, 2019, https://www.cnbc.com/2018/06/05/there-are-more-jobs-than-people-out-of-work.html.

63. Cox, Jeff, "There are more jobs than people out of work, something the American economy has never experienced before," CNBC Online, June 5, 2018, last accessed February 7, 2019, https://www.cnbc.com/2018/06/05/there-are-more-jobs-than-people-out-of-work.html.

64. Bedard, Paul, "Trump's list: 289 accomplishments in just 20 months, 'relentless' promise-keeping," The Washington Examiner Online, October 12, 2018, last accessed January 31, 2019, https://www.washingtonexaminer.com/washington-secrets/trumps-list-289-accomplishments-in-just-20-months-relentless-promise-keeping.

65. Bedard, Paul, "Trump's list: 289 accomplishments in just 20 months, 'relentless' promise-keeping," The Washington Examiner Online, October 12, 2018, last accessed January 31, 2019, https://www.washingtonexaminer.

com/washington-secrets/trumps-list-289-accomplishments-in-just-20-months-relentless-promise-keeping.

66. Bedard, Paul, "Trump's list: 289 accomplishments in just 20 months, 'relentless' promise-keeping," The Washington Examiner Online, October 12, 2018, last accessed January 31, 2019, https://www.washingtonexaminer.com/washington-secrets/trumps-list-289-accomplishments-in-just-20-months-relentless-promise-keeping.

67. "US weekly jobless claims near 49-year low; import prices fall," Fox News Online, December 13, 2018, last accessed Februaru 7, 2019, https://www.foxbusiness.com/economy/us-weekly-jobless-claims-near-49-year-low-import-prices-fall.

68. Trump, Donald, "Trump Administration Accomplishments," The White House Official Website, last accessed January 30, 2019. https://www.whitehouse.gov/trump-administration-accomplishments/.

69. Trump, Donald, "Trump Administration Accomplishments," The White House Official Website, last accessed January 30, 2019. https://www.whitehouse.gov/trump-administration-accomplishments/.

70. Bedard, Paul, "Trump's list: 289 accomplishments in just 20 months, 'relentless' promise-keeping," The Washington Examiner Online, October 12, 2018, last accessed January 31, 2019, https://www.washingtonexaminer.com/washington-secrets/trumps-list-289-accomplishments-in-just-20-months-relentless-promise-keeping.

71. Bedard, Paul, "Trump's list: 289 accomplishments in just 20 months, 'relentless' promise-keeping," The Washington Examiner Online, October 12, 2018, last accessed January 31, 2019, https://www.washingtonexaminer.com/washington-secrets/trumps-list-289-accomplishments-in-just-20-months-relentless-promise-keeping.

72. Bedard, Paul, "Trump's list: 289 accomplishments in just 20 months, 'relentless' promise-keeping," The Washington Examiner Online, October 12, 2018, last accessed January 31, 2019, https://www.washingtonexaminer.com/washington-secrets/trumps-list-289-accomplishments-in-just-20-months-relentless-promise-keeping.

73. Bedard, Paul, "Trump's list: 289 accomplishments in just 20 months, 'relentless' promise-keeping," The Washington Examiner Online, October 12, 2018, last accessed January 31, 2019, https://www.washingtonexaminer. com/washington-secrets/trumps-list-289-accomplishments-in-just-20- months-relentless-promise-keeping.

74. Bedard, Paul, "Trump's list: 289 accomplishments in just 20 months, 'relentless' promise-keeping," The Washington Examiner Online, October 12, 2018, last accessed January 31, 2019, https://www.washingtonexaminer. com/washington-secrets/trumps-list-289-accomplishments-in-just-20- months-relentless-promise-keeping.

75. Brandon, Adam, "Trump boom ignites small business," The Hill, June 25, 2018, last accessed February 7, 2019, https://thehill.com/opinion/ finance/393803-trump-boom-ignites-small-business.

76. Brandon, Adam, "Trump boom ignites small business," The Hill, June 25, 2018, last accessed February 7, 2019, https://thehill.com/opinion/ finance/393803-trump-boom-ignites-small-business.

77. Bedard, Paul, "Trump's list: 289 accomplishments in just 20 months, 'relentless' promise-keeping," The Washington Examiner Online, October 12, 2018, last accessed January 31, 2019, https://www.washingtonexaminer. com/washington-secrets/trumps-list-289-accomplishments-in-just-20- months-relentless-promise-keeping.

78. Brandon, Adam, "Trump boom ignites small business," The Hill, June 25, 2018, last accessed February 7, 2019, https://thehill.com/opinion/ finance/393803-trump-boom-ignites-small-business.

79. Trump, Donald, "Trump Administration Accomplishments," The White House Official Website, last accessed January 30, 2019. https://www. whitehouse.gov/trump-administration-accomplishments/.

80. Bedard, Paul, "Trump's list: 289 accomplishments in just 20 months, 'relentless' promise-keeping," The Washington Examiner Online, October 12, 2018, last accessed January 31, 2019, https://www.washingtonexaminer. com/washington-secrets/trumps-list-289-accomplishments-in-just-20- months-relentless-promise-keeping.

81. Bedard, Paul, "Trump's list: 289 accomplishments in just 20 months, 'relentless' promise-keeping," The Washington Examiner Online, October 12, 2018, last accessed January 31, 2019, https://www.washingtonexaminer.com/washington-secrets/trumps-list-289-accomplishments-in-just-20-months-relentless-promise-keeping.

82. Bedard, Paul, "Trump's list: 289 accomplishments in just 20 months, 'relentless' promise-keeping," The Washington Examiner Online, October 12, 2018, last accessed January 31, 2019, https://www.washingtonexaminer.com/washington-secrets/trumps-list-289-accomplishments-in-just-20-months-relentless-promise-keeping.

83. Grisales, Claudia, "Trump says 2020 defense budget will drop to $700 billion," Stars and Stripes Online, October 17, 2018, last accessed January 30, 2019, https://www.stripes.com/news/us/trump-says-2020-defense-budget-will-drop-to-700-billion-1.552276.

84. De Lea, Brittany, "Trump ups NATO contribution target as allies lag on defense spending," Fox Business Online, July 11, 2018, last accessed January 30, 2019, https://www.foxbusiness.com/politics/trump-ups-nato-contribution-target-as-allies-lag-on-defense-spending.

85. De Lea, Brittany, "Trump ups NATO contribution target as allies lag on defense spending," Fox Business Online, July 11, 2018, last accessed January 30, 2019, https://www.foxbusiness.com/politics/trump-ups-nato-contribution-target-as-allies-lag-on-defense-spending.

86. De Lea, Brittany, "Trump ups NATO contribution target as allies lag on defense spending," Fox Business Online, July 11, 2018, last accessed January 30, 2019, https://www.foxbusiness.com/politics/trump-ups-nato-contribution-target-as-allies-lag-on-defense-spending.

87. Tankersley, Jim & Bradsher, Keith, "Trump Hits China With Tariffs on $200 Billion in Goods, Escalating Trade War," The New York Times, September 17, 2019, last accessed January 31, 2019, https://www.nytimes.com/2018/09/17/us/politics/trump-china-tariffs-trade.html.

88. Davidson, Paul, "Trump trade war: Why he's fighting it and how tariffs work," USA Today Online, August 27, 2018, last accessed January

31, 2019, https://www.usatoday.com/story/money/2018/08/27/
trump-trade-war-tariffs-how-they-work/988027002/.

89. Lynch, David; Dawsey, Josh; and Paletta, Damian, "Trump imposes
    ssteel and aluminum tariffs on the E.U., Canada and Mexico," The
    Washington Post, May 31, 2018, last accessed January 31, 2019,
    https://www.washingtonpost.com/business/economy/trump-imposes-
    steel-and-aluminum-tariffs-on-the-european-union-canada-and-
    mexico/2018/05/31/891bb452-64d3-11e8-a69c-b944de66d9e7_story.
    html?utm_term=.c2f13057dd2f.

90. Sampathkumar, Mythili, "USMCA: What Donald Trump's Nafta
    replacement trade deal means and how it will work," Independent Online,
    October 2, 2018, last accessed January 31, 2019, https://www.independent.
    co.uk/news/world/americas/us-politics/usmca-nafta-trump-us-canada-trade-
    deal-what-mexico-trudeau-a8564211.html.

91. Katharine Lee Bates, "America, the Beautiful," 1913, USA Flag Site Online,
    last accessed March 22, 2017, http://www.usa-flag-site.org/song-lyrics/
    america/.

92. Kim Ghattas, "Obama and Clinton: A Special and Pragmatic Relationship,"
    July 6, 2017, BBC News Online, last accessed March 22, 2017, http://
    www.bbc.com/news/election-us-2016-36723216.

93. Matt Barber, "Agents Must Now Blow Whistle on Clinton/Obama
    Corruption," November 7, 2016, Townhall News Online, last accessed
    March 22, 2017, https://townhall.com/columnists/mattbarber/2016/11/07/
    agents-must-now-blow-whistle-on-clintonobama-corruption-n2242484.

94. Ibid.

95. Bob Eschliman, "WikiLeaks: Hillary Clinton Will Be
    Arrested," November 1, 2016, Charisma News Online, last
    accessed March 23, 2017, http://www.charismanews.com/
    politics/60951-wikileaks-hillary-clinton-will-be-arrested.

96. "The Role of the Supreme Court, Adapted from The Presidency, Congress,
    and the Supreme Court, Scholastic, Inc." 1989, Scholastic Inc. Online, last
    accessed March 22, 2017, https://www.scholastic.com/teachers/articles/
    teaching-content/role-supreme-court/.

97. Ariane de Vogue, "How the Supreme Court Has Changed Since Antonin Scalia Died," April 5, 2016, CNN Politics Online, last accessed March 22, 2017, http://www.cnn.com/2016/04/04/politics/supreme-court-scalia-eight-justices/.

98. Dan Mangan, "Trump: I'll Appoint Supreme Court Justices to Overturn Roe v. Wade Abortion Case," October 19, 2016, CNBC News Online, last accessed March 27, 2017, http://www.cnbc.com/2016/10/19/trump-ill-appoint-supreme-court-justices-to-overturn-roe-v-wade-abortion-case.html.

99. Kristi Hamrick, "AUL Calls on U.S. Senate to Confirm Judge Neil Gorsuch to U.S. Supreme Court," March 15, 2017, Christian Newswire Online, last accessed March 27, 2017, http://www.christiannewswire.com/index.php?module=releases&task=view&releaseID=79249.

100. Ian Millhiser, "An Historic Attempt to Kill Roe v. Wade May Backfire Spectacularly on the Anti-Choice Right," February 23, 2016, Think Progress Online, last accessed March 27, 2017, https://thinkprogress.org/an-historic-attempt-to-kill-roe-v-wade-may-backfire-spectacularly-on-the-anti-choice-right-e7d8ca923229#.wfe4n7oae.

101. Elving, Ron, "What Happened With Merrick Garland In 2016 And Why It Matters Now," NPR Online, June 29, 2018, last accessed February 4, 2018, https://www.npr.org/2018/06/29/624467256/what-happened-with-merrick-garland-in-2016-and-why-it-matters-now.

102. Shear, Michael D. "Supreme Court Justice Anthony Kennedy Will Retire," The New York Times, June 27, 2018, last accessed February 4, 2019, https://www.nytimes.com/2018/06/27/us/politics/anthony-kennedy-retire-supreme-court.html.

103. Wolf, Richard, "President Trump's conservative court shift may slow down as liberal judges avoid retirement," USA Today Online, November 19, 2018, last accessed January 30, 2019, https://www.usatoday.com/story/news/politics/2018/11/19/donald-trumps-judges-making-courts-more-conservative-slowly/2005281002/.

104. Wolf, Richard, "President Trump's conservative court shift may slow down as liberal judges avoid retirement," USA Today Online, November 19,

2018, last accessed January 30, 2019, https://www.usatoday.com/story/news/politics/2018/11/19/donald-trumps-judges-making-courts-more-conservative-slowly/2005281002/.

105. Foran, Clare, "The plan to overturn Roe v. Wade at the Supreme Court is already in motion," CNN Online, June 29, 2018, last accessed February 4, 2019, https://www.cnn.com/2018/06/29/politics/abortion-roe-v-wade-supreme-court/index.html.

106. Hausknecht, Bruce, "4 Reasons Why You Won't Like Brett Kavanaugh on the Supreme Court," 2018, last accessed February 4, 2019, https://www.focusonthefamily.com/socialissues/religious-freedom/4-reasons-why-you-wont-like-brett-kavanaugh-on-the-supreme-court.

107. Internal Revenue Service, "The Restriction of Political Campaign Intervention by Section 501(c)(3) Tax-Exempt Organizations," September 13, 2016, Internal Revenue Official Website, last accessed March 9, 2017, https://www.irs.gov/charities-non-profits/charitable-organizations/the-restriction-of-political-campaign-intervention-by-section-501-c-3-tax-exempt-organizations.

108. Internal Revenue Service, "Exemption Requirements—501(c)(3) Organizations," January 26, 2017, Internal Revenue Service Official Website, last accessed March 9, 2017, https://www.irs.gov/charities-non-profits/charitable-organizations/exemption-requirements-section-501-c-3-organizations.

109. Internal Revenue Service, "Lobbying," February 24, 2017, Internal Revenue Service Official Website, last accessed March 9, 2017, https://www.irs.gov/charities-non-profits/lobbying.

110. Internal Revenue Service, "Tax Guide for Churches and Religious Organizations Publication 1828, page 4," August 2015, Internal Revenue Official Website, last accessed on March 9, 2017, https://www.irs.gov/pub/irs-pdf/p1828.pdf.

111. Peter Kershaw, "501c3 Facts," Heal Our Land Ministries Online, last accessed March 9, 2017, http://hushmoney.org/501c3-facts.htm.

112. Christopher J. E. Johnson, "501c3: The Devil's Church," August

13, 2012, updated February 1, 2017, Creation Liberty Evangelism Online, last accessed March 9, 2017, http://www.creationliberty.com/articles/501c3.php.

113. Peter Kershaw, "501C3 Myths," June 14, 2004, "Heal Our Land Ministries Online," last accessed March 13, 2017, http://hushmoney.org/501c3-myths.htm.

114. Internal Revenue Service, "K. Voluntary Relinquishing of Tax Exempt Status," 1985, Internal Revenue Service Official Website, last accessed on March 14, 2017, https://www.irs.gov/pub/irs-tege/eotopick85.pdf.

115. Vega, Cecilia, "Trump signs executive order to ease restrictions on religious participation in politics," ABC News Online, May 4, 2017, last accessed February 4, 2019, https://abcnews.go.com/Politics/trump-signs-executive-order-ease-restrictions-religious-participation/story?id=47190000.

116. Vega, Cecilia, "Trump signs executive order to ease restrictions on religious participation in politics," ABC News Online, May 4, 2017, last accessed February 4, 2019, https://abcnews.go.com/Politics/trump-signs-executive-order-ease-restrictions-religious-participation/story?id=47190000.

117. Vega, Cecilia, "Trump signs executive order to ease restrictions on religious participation in politics," ABC News Online, May 4, 2017, last accessed February 4, 2019, https://abcnews.go.com/Politics/trump-signs-executive-order-ease-restrictions-religious-participation/story?id=47190000.

118. Valverde, Miriam, "Trump claims he got rid of the Johnson Amendment. Is that true?" Politifact Online, July 18, 2017, last accessed February 4, 2019, https://www.politifact.com/truth-o-meter/statements/2017/jul/18/donald-trump/trump-claims-he-got-rid-johnson-amendment-true/.

119. Vega, Cecilia, "Trump signs executive order to ease restrictions on religious participation in politics," ABC News Online, May 4, 2017, last accessed February 4, 2019, https://abcnews.go.com/Politics/

trump-signs-executive-order-ease-restrictions-religious-participation/
story?id=47190000.

120. "U.S. House of Representatives Votes To Repeal
Johnson Amendment," December 21, 2018, last
accessed February 4, 2019, https://www.ffcoalition.
com/u-s-house-of-representatives-votes-to-repeal-johnson-amendment/.

121. Gill, Benjamin, "House Passes Bill to Free Pastors from IRS Muzzle
and Shield Churches from Accidental New Tax," CBN News Online,
December 21, 2018, last accessed February 4, 2019, http://www1.cbn.
com/cbnnews/politics/2018/december/house-passes-bill-to-free-pastors-
from-irs-muzzle-and-shield-churches-from-accidental-new-tax.

122. News, Erisa, "House Passes H.R. 88 With Savings Provisions
Up for Senate Consideration," Ascensus Online, December
24, 2018, last accessed February 4, 2019, https://www2.
ascensus.com/news/industry-regulatory-news/2018/12/24/
house-passes-h-r-88-with-savings-provisions-up-for-senate-consideration/.

123. Clark,Charles, "Could President Trump Actually Have
Hillary Clinton Arrested?" Government Executive
Newsletters, November 11, 2016, last accessed February 8,
2019, https://www.govexec.com/management/2016/11/
could-president-trump-actually-have-hillary-clinton-arrested/133113/.

124. Clark,Charles, "Could President Trump Actually Have
Hillary Clinton Arrested?" Government Executive
Newsletters, November 11, 2016, last accessed February 8,
2019, https://www.govexec.com/management/2016/11/
could-president-trump-actually-have-hillary-clinton-arrested/133113/.

125. Yglesias, Matthew, "11House Republicans call for prosecutions
of Clinton, Comey, Lynch, and others," Vox Online,
April 18, 2018, last accessed February 8, 2019, https://
www.vox.com/policy-and-politics/2018/4/18/17252290/
desantis-letter-prosecute-clinton-comey.